THE GREAT IRISH POLITICS BOOK

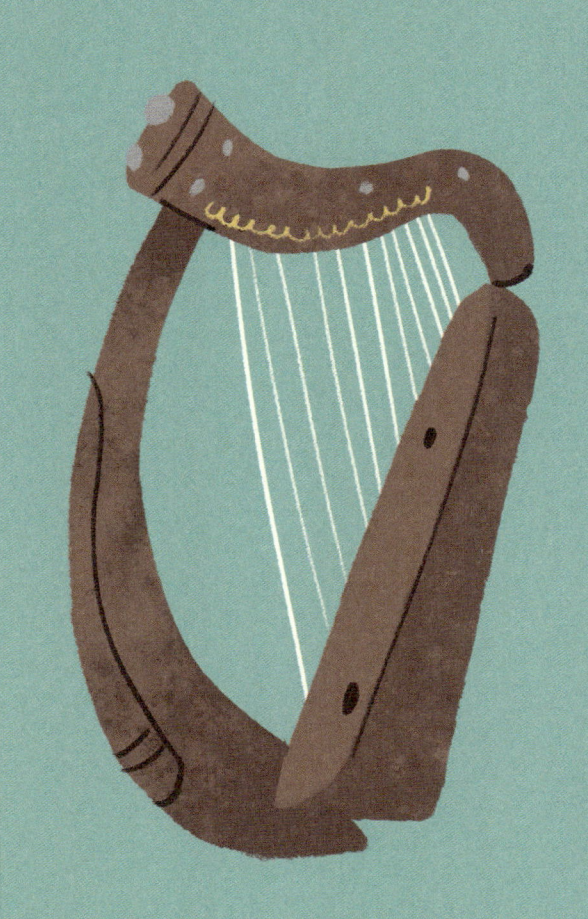

DAVID McCULLAGH

ILLUSTRATED BY GRAHAM CORCORAN

GILL BOOKS

ABOUT THE AUTHOR AND ILLUSTRATOR

David McCullagh is the author of several books. He began working as a journalist with the *Evening Press* before joining RTÉ, where he presented the broadcaster's flagship current affairs programme, *Prime Time*, before becoming an anchor on the *Six One* news. He is the author of the acclaimed books *The Reluctant Taoiseach*, *De Valera Rise* and *De Valera Rule*.

Graham Corcoran is an illustrator based in Dublin. He has previously illustrated two An Post Irish Book Award–nominated children's books, *Dare to Dream* by Sarah Webb and *The Story of Croke Park* by Mícheál Ó Muircheartaigh.

ACKNOWLEDGEMENTS

David: My thanks to everyone at Gill for suggesting this project, and for the ideas and comments which made it so much better – all errors are of course my own. To Graham Corcoran for bringing it alive. To my supportive bosses (Jon Williams, Hilary McGouran and Dave Nally). To my wife, Anne-Marie Smyth, and our daughter, Rosie, for their help, encouragement and support. And a special extra thanks to Anne-Marie and her colleagues on *news2Day* for their inspiration.

Graham: A huge thank you to Sarah, Aoibheann and all the team at Gill Books for the opportunity to work on this book. To David McCullagh for his brilliant and informative writing, I learned so much while illustrating these pages! To Graham Thew for his fantastic design skills. To my mum and dad for always encouraging my work. And to my wonderful wife, Nicole, for all her love and support.

CONTENTS

INTRODUCTION 2

HOW DID WE GET HERE? 4

WHO RUNS THE COUNTRY? 16

HOW DO WE ELECT OUR LEADERS? 32

HOW DO WE KEEP THE RULES? 40

WHY CAN'T WE AGREE? 56

WHAT ARE THE BIG ISSUES? 64

WHAT IS OUR PLACE IN THE WORLD? 80

INDEX 90

INTRODUCTION

WHAT DO WE MEAN WHEN WE TALK ABOUT POLITICS? IS IT LONG SPEECHES IN THE DÁIL THAT NO ONE IS LISTENING TO? OR PEOPLE SHOUTING OVER EACH OTHER IN TELEVISION STUDIOS? THAT DOESN'T SOUND LIKE SOMETHING THAT MIGHT AFFECT *YOU*.

But politics is about more than that – it's about *how* decisions are made, it's about *what* decisions are made, and it's about *who* makes the decisions. And it doesn't have to be politicians making those decisions – it can be a group of friends.

The government might decide big things, like whether a country should go to war or how much tax people should pay. But you and your friends or family might have to make decisions too, like what computer game to play or what time to have dinner.

Our lives are all about choices – small ones as well as big ones – and when we make choices that affect other people as well as ourselves, we have to agree how to make them and who should make them. And that is politics.

The results of those choices are all around us. For instance, how you get to school in the morning depends on all sorts of decisions. You might be able to walk – *if* you live close to the school. You might be able to cycle – *if* the local council has built cycle lanes to make it safe. You might get the bus – *if* the government spent money on public transport. Or you might go in the car – *if* your family has one.

And the decision you make on how to get to school affects lots of other things. If you walk or cycle, you'll be fitter than if you take the bus or the car. If you take the car, there will be more traffic jams on the road and your journey will do more damage to the environment. If you take the bus, it will cost you more than walking. We all make choices, all the time, and those decisions affect other people as well as ourselves.

Who gets to make those decisions if they affect more than one person? The answer will be different for each group. In a family, your parents usually make the decisions. In the classroom, the teacher will decide. On a sports team, the captain calls the shots. These people all have **AUTHORITY** – all or most members of the group agree to let them decide things.

But what about a country? Usually, in a country the **GOVERNMENT** has authority. It will decide what to do, and the people, or most of them, will follow that decision. In a democracy, the government is chosen by the people, who can criticise its decisions. And if enough people don't like how the government does things, they can change the government – usually in an election.

Why do we need a government in the first place? Some people think we don't, that people could get along fine without one. But many others think that if there was no government, no state and no laws, then things would be worse, especially for those with less power, who might be treated unfairly by the more powerful.

A famous thinker called Thomas Hobbes said that without a central authority that everyone accepted, life would be 'nasty, brutish and short'. Which sounds like a description of someone I used to know. But what Hobbes meant was that without rules that were enforced, everyone would be fighting all the time to get what they needed to survive – food, water, shelter – and nobody would live very long.

The way Hobbes saw it, in society we all agree to do two things. First, we give up some of our freedom to make our own decisions – we *share* decision-making. Second, we agree to obey the decisions made by the group. The result, hopefully, is that everyone is safer, happier and better off.

Usually, we can get more done if we co-operate. Say your cat has got stuck in a tall tree. On your own, there's not much you can do about it – the cat is too scared to jump and too high up for you to reach. But if some friends help you by lifting you, you might be able to reach the cat and bring it down to safety. Co-operation makes things easier, and we can get more done.

And that's what we do in society. It would be impossible for each of us on our own, or even each family, to provide schools, and hospitals, and bus services, and all the other things we need. But by co-operating, each of us can do a small bit of the work, and we all benefit.

In this book, we're going to look at how decisions are made in this country, how our political system works, and what makes it different to other countries'. We'll also look at different ways of thinking about how society should be organised, at the big questions facing the country, and at how you can change things.

We're going to find out how Ireland works.

HOW DID WE GET HERE?

There are lots of different ways of running a country – you can give one person the power to make all the decisions, or you can allow everyone to have their say. You can have a separate government for each nation, or you can have an empire that has one government for lots of different nations. Central government can decide everything, or it can share power with local governments at state or county level.

Ireland is a republic and a democracy. This means that the power to decide comes from the people who live here. The voters get to choose the government and to decide on big issues that face the country.

But that wasn't always our political system. Over the centuries, there have been different ways of governing Ireland. In Gaelic times, each clan had its own king. Later the country was ruled by Britain, and that country's king or queen (known as the **MONARCH**) was in charge.

Gradually the monarch became less powerful, and decisions were made in the British parliament. This was more democratic, but not completely democratic because only some people were allowed to vote. And people in Ireland didn't have much of a say because they were a small minority in the overall United Kingdom, with only around 100 of the 600 members of parliament.

It was only after independence that Irish people were able to make all the decisions about what happened in this country. And it was only then that all adults were allowed to vote, giving everyone a say.

Looking at our own history gives us a chance to explore different ways of running a country and to see which system you think is best!

IRELAND'S POLITICAL SYSTEM: CLANS

LONG AGO, IN GAELIC IRELAND, SOCIETY WAS ORGANISED ON THE BASIS OF EXTENDED FAMILIES, CALLED CLANS ('CLANN' IS THE IRISH WORD FOR 'FAMILY') OR SEPTS. THE CLAN OCCUPIED A PARTICULAR AREA, THEIR DÚICHE ('ANCESTRAL LAND', 'NATIVE PLACE' OR 'HOME COUNTRY').

Clan members shared a surname, which indicated an ancestor they had in common. For instance, the grandchildren of the famous king Brian Boru called themselves Ó Briain, showing that they were descended from him. In the same way, the O'Neills were supposed to be descendants of Niall, the O'Donnells of Domhnal, and so on.

CLAN LEADERS

Each clan had a chief (taoiseach) or king. Several clans together were ruled by an overking, who in turn owed loyalty to the provincial king. The five provinces were Ulaidh (Ulster), Laighin (Leinster), Mumhain (Munster), Midhe (Meath) and Connacht. Usually, but not always, there was a recognised high king who ruled the entire island.

The clans elected their taoiseach or king, as well as a deputy or tánaiste, a relative who would automatically succeed whenever the leader died. Only members of the most important and powerful families were elected to be leaders. There were also meetings at each level to agree laws – kings weren't able to do whatever they wanted without agreement.

SOCIAL RANK

In Gaelic society, warriors were important because the different clans were often at war with each other. But poets were important too (partly because, in a time before writing, their poems were a way of remembering traditions and laws). Gaelic Ireland had its own distinctive legal system, known as the Brehon laws, and lawyers were important too.

But most people weren't kings, or poets, or lawyers. Gaelic Ireland had different social levels – although, unlike in some other societies, it was possible to move up or down the ranks. The kings and their immediate families were at the top, with the people doing important jobs, like doctors, lawyers, musicians or craftsmen, at the next level. Then there were freemen who owned land, followed by landless freemen and finally slaves. People became slaves either as punishment for a crime or after being captured from another clan during a war. And guess who did most of the work?

The Gaelic political system was gradually destroyed after the Norman invasion from England in 1169. It survived at first outside the areas controlled by the Normans (and later by the English Crown). But when the last Gaelic leaders left the country in 1607 after being beaten in battle, English control was complete and the old society died out.

BREHON LAWS

The Brehon laws give us hints about how the people of Gaelic Ireland thought about crime, property and marriage.

Because there were no prisons, people who committed crimes had to pay fines rather than be locked up – even for murder. But if the fine wasn't paid, a murderer could be put to death. Often, the fine had to be paid by the criminal's family – so everyone had an interest in making sure their relatives didn't break the law.

- If you hit someone hard enough to raise a lump, but without causing the victim to bleed, you would have to pay a fine of two cows.

- If a pregnant woman asked her husband for food and he didn't give it to her, he had to pay a fine.

- A husband or wife could decide they wanted to end their marriage – but only if they announced their decision on a particular day, 1 February.

- If a marriage ended, the woman was entitled to keep whatever property she had brought to the marriage.

- Families were required to give their elderly parents one oatcake and a container of sour milk every day.

- A monk was only allowed three pints of ale with his lunch (other people were allowed six pints) so he would be sober when saying prayers.

IRELAND'S POLITICAL SYSTEM: MONARCHY

UNDER ENGLISH RULE, IRELAND WAS A MONARCHY – IT WAS RULED BY QUEENS OR KINGS. IN A MONARCHY, ONE PERSON HAS THE FINAL SAY IN ALL DECISIONS, AND THAT PERSON IS THE ONE WEARING THE CROWN.

Usually, monarchs rule for life, and the job is **HEREDITARY**, which means that when they die, their son or daughter or another relative becomes the next monarch.

The idea of monarchy has usually been closely related to religion. In ancient Egypt, people believed their monarch, the pharaoh, was an actual god. In more recent times, people believed in the **DIVINE RIGHT OF KINGS**, the idea that the monarch's power came from God.

Until 1801, Ireland was a separate kingdom with its own parliament. In that year, the Act of Union abolished the Irish parliament and created the United Kingdom of Great Britain and Ireland. From then on, Irish members of parliament (MPs) went to the British House of Commons in London.

Between 1728 and 1793, Catholics weren't allowed to vote at all, and they were banned for even longer from holding important jobs or from sitting in parliament. In order to vote, people had to own a certain amount of property, but the right to vote was gradually extended to more and more people – to about 16 per cent of men under the 1850 Reform Act, increasing to 50 per cent in 1884. The secret ballot was introduced in 1872 – before that, people voted in public and could come under pressure (for instance, from their landlords) to vote a certain way.

THE PEOPLE HAVE THEIR SAY

But while most people didn't have a vote, that didn't mean they didn't have a voice, and Daniel O'Connell created one of the world's first popular mass movements. He showed the government that the people were with him by holding massive public rallies, known as **MONSTER MEETINGS**. In 1829, after a huge campaign led by O'Connell, the government removed the ban on Catholics being MPs. But his attempt to repeal the Act of Union and re-establish a separate Irish parliament failed.

O'Connell was happy to keep the British monarch if Ireland had its own parliament. But others had more radical ideas.

After the American War of Independence and the French Revolution a new idea became popular – republicanism, which said Ireland should be ruled, not by a monarch, but by representatives of the people.

People who believed Ireland should be a republic called themselves the United Irishmen because they wanted to overcome the divisions between different religious groups in the country.

ABSOLUTE POWER CORRUPTS ABSOLUTELY

Giving somebody unlimited power can lead to some very strange decisions.

- **Roman emperor Caligula suggested making his favourite horse a consul (a senior lawmaker) – though his comment may have been meant as a joke at the expense of the existing consuls.**

- **Russian tsar Peter the Great banned beards and moustaches – if people refused to shave, they had to pay a tax on their facial hair.**

- **King Frederick William I of Prussia had a collection – of extra-tall soldiers. The king, who was himself 5 feet 3 inches tall, watched his Potsdam Giants train every day. They included Irishman James Kirkland, who was 7 feet 1 inch tall.**

IRELAND'S POLITICAL SYSTEM: REPUBLIC

THE UNITED IRISHMEN WERE DEFEATED IN THE 1798 REBELLION, BUT THEIR IDEAS BECAME CENTRAL TO THE INDEPENDENCE MOVEMENT – PEOPLE CAME TO THINK THAT IRELAND SHOULD NOT JUST BE FREE OF BRITAIN, IT SHOULD ALSO BE A DEMOCRATIC REPUBLIC.

Republicanism inspired the 1916 Easter Rising against British rule. In the 1918 general election, the Sinn Féin party won a large majority of Ireland's seats in the British parliament. They refused to go to London to take their seats, though, and set up their own parliament, Dáil Éireann, instead.

The struggle with British authority led to the War of Independence, which ended in a truce in July 1921. A treaty was agreed that December that set up the Irish Free State in 26 of the 32 counties. There was a separate parliament in the six counties of Northern Ireland, which remained part of the United Kingdom.

THE CIVIL WAR

The Irish Free State officially came into existence on 6 December 1922. The new state had its own parliament, which could make most of the decisions about what happened in Ireland. The British parliament at Westminster no longer made laws that affected what went on in the Irish Free State.

But Ireland still wasn't a republic. The treaty with Britain said that Irish people would continue to be subjects of the British Crown. Many republicans didn't like this, and there was a civil war between those who refused to give their loyalty to the British king and those who argued that the Irish Free State would, in time, be able to break the link with the Crown.

The main leader on the anti-treaty side was Éamon de Valera; the leader of the pro-treaty army was Michael Collins. Collins was killed in an ambush during the civil war at the age of just 31.

De Valera survived the civil war, though he was put in prison afterwards. Military defeat convinced him that the only way to achieve his aims was through peaceful politics, and he became the most successful politician in Irish history – head of government for 21 years and president for another 14.

AN INDEPENDENT IRELAND

After independence, the legal and political links with Britain were gradually loosened. In 1937, a new constitution removed all mention of the Crown and got rid of the name 'Irish Free State'. From then on, the state was called Ireland, or Éire, and was a republic in all but name.

Ireland stayed out of the Second World War, which annoyed the British but proved that Ireland was truly independent and could do whatever it wanted. In 1949, it officially left the British Commonwealth, and the description of the state was changed to the Republic of Ireland. This removed any confusion about whether or not Ireland was truly independent of Britain.

IRELAND'S FLAG

The tricolour is the national flag of Ireland. It was first flown publicly in Waterford in 1848 by Thomas Francis Meagher. It was inspired by the tricolour of revolutionary France, and the colours represent Catholics (green) and Protestants (orange) and the hoped-for unity between them (white).

NORTHERN IRELAND

POLITICS WORKS BEST WHEN MOST PEOPLE AGREE ON THE BASIC RULES – LIKE HOW WE DECIDE WHO GETS TO RUN THE COUNTRY OR WHAT COUNTRY WE SHOULD EVEN BE PART OF. BUT FOR MOST OF THE PAST HUNDRED YEARS, THAT HASN'T BEEN THE CASE IN NORTHERN IRELAND.

NATIONALISTS AND UNIONISTS

When the rest of the island became independent from Britain in 1922, six of the 32 counties, in the north-east, remained in the United Kingdom. This was because a majority of people in that area were **UNIONISTS**, who wanted to remain with Britain, rather than **NATIONALISTS**, who wanted Ireland to be independent.

But not everyone in Northern Ireland was a Unionist. In fact, about one-third of the people in the six counties were Nationalists, and that proportion has increased, so now the two sides are about even. The Nationalists in Northern Ireland never accepted the new arrangement, and they were treated badly by the Unionists, who were constantly in government. Nationalists had worse housing, fewer jobs and less educational opportunity.

Between 1969 and 1994, there was violence between Unionists and Nationalists and between Nationalists and the British Army. This period was known as **THE TROUBLES**, and it led to the deaths of over 3,600 people and injuries to many more. Terrible things were done by all sides in the conflict, and there was a lot of bitterness and hatred. Eventually, a deal was made to bring peace to Northern Ireland. The **GOOD FRIDAY AGREEMENT** of 1998 set up a new type of government, in which power is shared between Unionists and Nationalists.

THE NORTHERN IRELAND ASSEMBLY

The Northern Ireland Assembly is elected by proportional representation using a single transferable vote, or PR-STV (see page 36). Members can describe themselves as Unionist, Nationalist or neither. Some votes need support from both Unionists and Nationalists to pass.

The Assembly elects the government, called the Executive, which has a First Minister, nominated by the biggest party, and a Deputy First Minister, nominated by the second biggest party. All parties in the Assembly get to nominate ministers, depending on how many seats they have. So the parties have to share power.

The British and Irish governments have both agreed to respect the wishes of the people of Northern Ireland about whether it stays in the United Kingdom or becomes part of a united Ireland. Whatever happens, the two governments have promised to respect the rights of both communities.

'IRELAND'S CALL'

Most sports teams were set up before Ireland was divided between north and south. So when Irish people play rugby, or hockey, or cricket, the members come from both sides of the border. Sometimes the politics can be tricky – particularly around the singing of national anthems before matches. For rugby, it was agreed that the Irish national anthem, 'Amhrán na bhFiann', would be sung before matches in Dublin and 'God Save the Queen' before matches in Belfast. For a time, no anthem was sung at away matches. For the 1995 Rugby World Cup in South Africa, a new neutral anthem, 'Ireland's Call', was written, and this has been adopted by some other sports associations as well.

DEMOCRACY IN IRELAND TODAY

WE'VE SEEN HOW IRELAND CAME TO BE AN INDEPENDENT DEMOCRATIC REPUBLIC. BEFORE WE GO ON TO LOOK AT HOW THE POLITICAL SYSTEM WORKS, LET'S TAKE A CLOSER LOOK AT HOW OUR VERSION OF DEMOCRACY DIFFERS FROM SOME OTHERS'.

First of all, in our democracy, every adult is allowed to vote. This wasn't always the case. In Ireland and Britain before 1918, only some people – men aged 21 or over – could vote, and only if they owned a certain amount of property. No women **AT ALL** had the vote.

That changed in 1918, when all men aged over 21 got the vote. After a long struggle, some women finally won the right to vote too – but only if they were aged 30 or over and if they or their husbands owned a certain amount of property.

In the newly independent Irish Free State, all women gained the right to vote in 1922. This was six years before Britain. In France, women didn't get the vote until 1945, while in Switzerland this didn't happen until 1971!

The voting age was lowered to 18 in 1972.

DIRECT OR REPRESENTATIVE?

We have a **REPRESENTATIVE** democracy. In the first democracy, in Ancient Greece, democracy was 'direct', with decisions on new laws made by a meeting of everyone who was entitled to vote. This direct democracy worked because few people were allowed to vote and the decisions weren't that complicated.

But as society developed, states got bigger and governments did more, too many decisions had to be made too often for the people to decide directly on everything. So instead, the people chose **REPRESENTATIVES** to make the decisions for them – like when you elect a class rep in school.

But once representatives are elected, do they have to do exactly what the voters say? Some argue that they should, that they are delegates who should represent the views of their constituents. Others say they should make up their own mind on the issues – the voters have chosen them to use their own judgement to decide.

DEMOCRATIC SYSTEMS

Ireland has a **PARLIAMENTARY** system, where people elect representatives (TDs) to the parliament (Dáil), which then elects a head of government (the Taoiseach) who is responsible for running the country. The Taoiseach is responsible to the Dáil, and if they lose the support of a majority of TDs, they will be replaced. We also have a president, who is head of state, the symbolic figurehead who is the face of the country to the rest of the world, but *not* head of government.

In a **PRESIDENTIAL** system, like in the United States, the President is both head of government *and* head of state. There is also a parliament (in the US it's called Congress, made up of the Senate and the House of Representatives) that passes laws.

Ireland also has a **UNITARY** system, where the national government has most of the power. While some things are done by local government (councils or mayors), most of the important decisions are made at the centre.

In **FEDERAL** systems, like Germany, Australia or the United States of America, power is shared between the central government and governments in provinces or states. Local governments have a lot of power to do things, including raising money through taxes and deciding how to spend it, while the national government looks after things that can't be done at a local level – like dealing with other countries, running the army and making sure the regional governments treat everyone fairly.

DO AS I SAY – OR ELSE!

Dictatorship is a system where one person makes all the rules – that person tells people what to do, and they are not allowed to disagree. Many dictatorships still have some of the things you find in a democracy – like courts, or a parliament, or newspapers and television stations. But none of these things are independent of the government – they can't criticise the dictator or stop them doing whatever they want. All dictatorships have one thing in common: they are very difficult to get rid of. Because once a dictator has control, he likes to keep it (and, yes, it is almost always a man).

In some countries, the army has taken control of government – this is known as a military dictatorship. In others, parties have won elections, and then abolished elections to make sure they keep power.

A very extreme type of dictatorship is known as a totalitarian state, where the government doesn't just make people do what it wants, it also tries to force them to think the way it wants.

DIRECT: I want a vote in every decision the government makes.

REPRESENTATIVE: But there are dozens of decisions to be made every day – I don't have time for that!

But if you don't decide yourself, it's not a real democracy.

But I can choose someone to make the decisions for me – someone I trust.

You can't be sure they'll make the decision you want on every single issue.

No, but if I pick a good representative, they'll put in the time to find out all the important information and make a decision in my best interests.

That's like getting someone else to do your thinking for you!

No, it's like getting someone qualified to do a job I don't have the time for.

WHO RUNS THE COUNTRY?

We found out in the last section that Ireland is a representative democracy. So who are our representatives, and what do they do?

First of all, we have a parliament, the Oireachtas, made up of the Dáil and Seanad. We elect the members of the Dáil, called TDs. Then the TDs choose a government, led by the Taoiseach and made up of ministers, who are helped by civil servants.

The government, as long as it has the support of the Oireachtas, makes decisions about what happens in lots of different areas. It decides what is taught in schools, which side of the road we drive on and where a new hospital should be built. It decides how much money should be spent on doing all those things, and it decides where to get the money to pay for it all.

Then there are local authorities, councils that look after smaller areas like counties and cities.

And there is also a head of state, called the President, who represents the country at home and abroad.

All of these politicians work together to run the country. Sometimes they argue – in fact, they usually argue quite a lot. Sometimes people complain that the politicians have forgotten they are supposed to be working for the voters. And sometimes politicians make mistakes.

But they know that if they don't live up to their promises, or if they forget about the interests of the voters, they are likely to be reminded pretty quickly at the next election, when they could end up out of a job.

LEINSTER HOUSE

THE DÁIL AND TDS

THE **PARLIAMENT** OR **LEGISLATURE** IS THE PART OF THE POLITICAL SYSTEM THAT MAKES LAWS, ALSO KNOWN AS LEGISLATION. IN IRELAND, THE LEGISLATURE OR PARLIAMENT IS CALLED THE **OIREACHTAS**. BEFORE NEW LAWS COME INTO FORCE, THEY HAVE TO BE **PASSED** (AGREED TO BY A MAJORITY) BY BOTH HOUSES OF THE OIREACHTAS – THE DÁIL AND THE SEANAD – AND **SIGNED** BY THE PRESIDENT.

In our system, the parliament also has another very important job – keeping an eye on how those in power are doing their job, sometimes called **HOLDING GOVERNMENT TO ACCOUNT**. The government is elected by the Dáil and can only stay in power if it keeps the support of a majority of TDs. It can be removed if it loses a special vote, called a **VOTE OF CONFIDENCE**. If the government, or a minister, loses a vote of confidence, they have to resign. If the Dáil can't elect a new government to take its place, there is a general election.

THE CEANN COMHAIRLE

A member of the Dáil is called a TD, or Teachta Dála. One of the things they do is have debates in the Dáil chamber. The debates can get a bit heated if people get angry. Someone needs to keep control – just like a referee in a match. In the Dáil, the referee or chair is called the Ceann Comhairle, who keeps control of proceedings – or tries to. Sometimes TDs get over-excited and start shouting at each other, at which point the Ceann Comhairle might complain that they are behaving like children. This is very unfair – to children, who usually know how to take turns.

The Ceann Comhairle is seated at the centre of the horseshoe-shaped Dáil chamber, which has rows of seats rising from the floor. The Taoiseach sits to the Ceann Comhairle's left, with their ministers beside them on the front bench. The leader of the opposition (the head of the biggest party that isn't in government) sits across from the Taoiseach, on the Ceann Comhairle's right. They also have a front bench, the leading figures in their party who are each responsible for keeping an eye on a particular minister. Other TDs sit in seats further back, which is why they are called **BACKBENCHERS**. In politics, the word 'seat' means more than a place to sit – it refers to a place in parliament. So winning a seat in the Dáil or Seanad means being elected and a 3-seat constituency means an area that elects 3 TDs.

COMMITTEES

If you look at the Dáil on television, it can sometimes look pretty empty. If routine legislation is being discussed, only a couple of TDs might be present – a government representative and the opposition spokesperson on the issue involved. So where are the rest of the TDs? Most of them are probably in their offices, where they can keep an eye on the television to see what's going on in the chamber while dealing with emails and letters from voters who want them to do something, or reading up on proposed legislation, or writing speeches.

Or they could be at one of the committees that meet at the same time as the Dáil. Each government department has a committee that discusses legislation proposed by the minister concerned, as well as various important issues being dealt with by the department. For instance, the education committee might call in experts to discuss problems in schools, such as whether textbooks are up to scratch or how to improve the Leaving Cert.

OUT OF ORDER

What TDs say in the Dáil is protected by privilege – they cannot be sued over anything they say in the chamber. This is designed to allow them to bring important matters to public attention that otherwise would remain secret for fear of legal action. In this way, TDs have been able to bring scandals to light.

But that doesn't mean TDs can say anything they like – under the rules of the House, they are not allowed to call each other names. Nobody reading this book would call anyone else names, of course, but just in case, here are some of the names you are not allowed to call people in the Dáil: brat, buffoon, chancer, communist, corner boy, coward, fascist, gurrier, guttersnipe, hypocrite, rat, scumbag or yahoo.

MINISTERS

WE HEAR A LOT OF TALK ABOUT 'THE GOVERNMENT' – BUT WHAT IS IT, AND WHAT DOES IT DO?

The government is the name we give to the politicians who run the country, the ones with the power to make decisions about what happens in lots of different areas. The government (also known as the cabinet) is made up of the Taoiseach and up to 14 ministers.

Nearly all ministers are TDs – the Taoiseach can appoint up to two senators (members of the Seanad) to be ministers, but this doesn't happen very often. One minister is appointed Tánaiste, the deputy or second in command to the Taoiseach. This could be a senior member of the Taoiseach's own party or the leader of the second biggest party in a coalition (a government made up of more than one political party).

GOVERNMENT DEPARTMENTS

Each minister is responsible for a government department that deals with a particular area – education, for instance, or health, or finance. The minister sets out what the department should be trying to achieve; brings laws through the Oireachtas and tries to get money for their department; answers questions in the Dáil and in the media about what their department is doing; and is the voice and the face of the department. As well as cabinet ministers, there are also **MINISTERS OF STATE** or **JUNIOR MINISTERS** who are appointed to help run the departments. Most of them don't go to cabinet meetings, and they have fewer powers and less influence than senior ministers.

A minister might be in charge of a department, and be responsible for it to the Dáil, but they can't do all the work themselves. They have to rely on civil servants, the permanent staff of the department, who stay in the job even when there is a change of government. Each department is headed by a secretary-general, who works closely with their minister on the work of the department, giving advice and making sure decisions are followed. While the minister is responsible for **POLICY** – the overall direction of what the department does – the secretary-general is responsible for **ADMINISTRATION** – making sure the system works.

COLLECTIVE RESPONSIBILITY

Really big decisions have to be taken by the government as a whole, not just by the minister concerned. This might stop a minister from doing everything they want in their own department, but it also allows them to have a say in what their colleagues are up to. For example, imagine the Minister for Education decides to ban homework (hurrah!). This will need a law that has to be approved by government and passed by both the Dáil and Seanad before being signed by the President.

The first step is for the civil servants in the Department of Education to write a proposal, which is sent to each minister and then discussed at a cabinet meeting. Different ministers might have objections or suggestions, based either on the views of their departments or their own personal opinions. The Minister for Justice, for instance, might be advised by their officials that kids could get into trouble with the law if they weren't kept busy with homework. Or another minister might think that banning homework would be unpopular with parents – who, unlike schoolchildren, are able to vote.

So the issue will be discussed around the cabinet table and a decision reached. And once the decision is made, ministers have to support it in public – even if they disagreed with it! This is called **COLLECTIVE RESPONSIBILITY**. It means that every minister has to stick to what is agreed at cabinet, whatever their personal views. If they are so strongly opposed to the proposal that they can't support it, they have to resign.

Government discussions are also supposed to be secret – this is called **CABINET CONFIDENTIALITY**. The argument for this is that ministers will be able to have a better discussion, looking at all the angles of a decision, if what they say is kept private.

WHAT IS IN THE CABINET?

Another name for the government is the 'cabinet', a word which usually means a type of cupboard. But it also used to mean a small room, and that is where its political meaning comes from. In the days when kings made all the decisions, they got advice from senior officials in private – or 'in cabinet', meaning in a small room where no one else could hear them.

THE TAOISEACH

EVERY TEAM NEEDS A CAPTAIN, A LEADER, SOMEONE RESPONSIBLE FOR KEEPING EVERYONE WORKING TOGETHER. SOMETIMES A TEAM CAPTAIN WILL MAKE ALL THE DECISIONS, SOMETIMES A MAJORITY OF THE MEMBERS WILL DECIDE – BUT IT'S UP TO THE CAPTAIN TO MAKE SURE THE WHOLE TEAM KEEPS TO THE DECISIONS MADE.

Government is no different, and in Ireland, the leader of the government is the Taoiseach. Every country with a parliamentary system has a similar top job, usually known as 'prime minister'. The word 'taoiseach' comes from Gaelic times and translates as 'chieftain', so *our* prime minister has a much more exciting title than the others.

HOW DO YOU BECOME TAOISEACH?

The Taoiseach is appointed by the President, after being nominated by the Dáil. In other words, to become Taoiseach, you have to have the support of a majority of TDs. After this Dáil vote, the new Taoiseach goes to Áras an Uachtaráin, the President's residence, to be formally appointed, and then returns to the Dáil to announce the ministers who will be responsible for each department. This group of top players is called the government, or the cabinet. If a Taoiseach resigns or loses a vote of confidence, the government comes to an end, though the members remain in their jobs until successors are appointed by the Dáil.

WHAT DOES THE TAOISEACH DO?

The Taoiseach is in charge of cabinet meetings, deciding who gets to speak and in what order, which gives them a lot of control over how the discussion goes and what decision is reached. The Taoiseach decides who becomes a minister and for which department. While lots of politicians might fancy their chances of getting the top job themselves, they have to be careful not to get on the wrong side of the Taoiseach, who, like any captain, can drop them from the team.

To the public and in the media, the Taoiseach is the face of the government, the one who makes important announcements, leads debates in the Dáil and gets to have the final word in disagreements. It is – by far – the most powerful job in government and in Irish politics.

Does this mean the Taoiseach can do whatever they want? Not quite. For starters, every Irish government since 1989 has been a *coalition*, made up of more than one political party. If a Taoiseach decided to do something the other party or parties opposed, it could lead to the collapse of the government. Even within the Taoiseach's own party, some TDs might be opposed to a particular decision – and no leader wants to split their own party if they can help it. No Taoiseach can afford to ignore what the public thinks of what they are doing either. After all, most politicians want to stay in power, which means winning the next election.

No matter how powerful the job is, the Taoiseach, just like every successful politician, has to learn to compromise and to persuade people to come along – internal party critics, coalition partners and the public. If they don't manage to do that, then they won't be Taoiseach for very long.

SO YOU WANT TO BE TAOISEACH?

Game board:

- 64: CONGRATULATIONS! YOU ARE TAOISEACH
- 61: SOCIAL MEDIA POSTS FROM YOUR PAST COME BACK TO HAUNT YOU
- 53: YOU WIN A TELEVISED DEBATE
- 51: CONGRATULATIONS! YOU ARE THE LEADER OF THE OPPOSITION
- 45: YOU MAKE A PROMISE YOU CAN'T KEEP
- 43: YOU CHALLENGE THE TAOISEACH FOR LEADERSHIP – AND LOSE!
- 41: CONGRATULATIONS! YOU ARE A MINISTER
- 34: YOU SOLVE A DIFFICULT PROBLEM – AND GET THE CREDIT
- 31: CONGRATULATIONS! YOU ARE A JUNIOR MINISTER
- 26: YOUR RUNNING MATE TAKES YOUR SEAT
- 25: YOUR RUNNING MATE IS ELECTED
- 21: CONGRATULATIONS! YOU ARE A TD
- 18: FIRST TV APPEARANCE – YOU WERE TERRIBLE
- 19: FIRST TV APPEARANCE – YOU WERE GREAT
- 14: YOU GET A NEW PARK BUILT
- 11: CONGRATULATIONS! YOU ARE A COUNCILLOR
- 10: RIVAL STEALS YOUR POSTERS!
- 4: YOU ARE PICKED TO RUN IN THE LOCAL ELECTIONS
- 1: START

Tokens: JACK LYNCH, SEÁN LEMASS, W.T. COSGRAVE, ÉAMON DE VALERA

THE SEANAD

THE SECOND HOUSE OF THE OIREACHTAS IS THE SEANAD. IT IS SOMETIMES CALLED **THE UPPER HOUSE**, EVEN THOUGH IT HAS LESS POWER THAN THE DÁIL. IT DOES NOT ELECT THE GOVERNMENT, AND WHILE IT CAN DELAY LAWS IT DOESN'T LIKE, IT CAN'T STOP THEM COMPLETELY – IF THERE IS A DISAGREEMENT, THE DÁIL CAN OVERRULE THE SEANAD.

And, unlike the Dáil, the Seanad isn't directly elected by all voters. Instead, senators are elected by other politicians or by university graduates, or are appointed by the Taoiseach. This is deliberate – the Seanad is not supposed to be a rival to the Dáil in terms of importance or power.

WHY DO WE NEED THE SEANAD?

There was a referendum on whether we needed a second house of the Oireachtas in 2013. Even though politicians aren't always popular, and abolishing the Seanad would have put 60 of them out of a job, voters decided to keep it. They thought it was worth keeping, not as a rival to the Dáil, but as an extra set of eyes on new laws. Sometimes the Seanad spots mistakes in legislation and is able to correct them before they become law.

Out of the 60 Senators, 11 are appointed by the Taoiseach, 6 are elected by university graduates and 43 are elected on what are called **VOCATIONAL PANELS**.

VOCATIONAL PANELS

When the Seanad was being designed in the 1930s, there was a fashionable theory that people should be represented in parliament through their jobs rather than where they happened to live. So a farmer in Carlow should vote for someone to represent farmers, rather than someone to represent the constituency, or voting area, of Carlow–Kilkenny. And a shop owner in Limerick should vote for someone to represent businesses, rather than Limerick City.

This idea was partly used in designing the Seanad, with the vocational panels supposed to represent different areas of Irish life. The panels are: Administrative (7 seats), Agricultural (11 seats), Cultural and Educational (5 seats), Industrial and Commercial (9 seats) and Labour (11 seats). To qualify to run for a panel, candidates have to have 'knowledge and practical experience' of the area it covers.

You might imagine that this would mean that the farmers' organisations would fill the Agricultural panel, teachers would dominate the Cultural and Educational panel, and business groups would hold the seats on the Industrial and Commercial panel. But guess who decides how the Seanad is elected? That's right, politicians. And they decided to give the power to elect senators to … themselves!

WHO ELECTS THE SEANAD?

The vocational panels are elected by TDs, outgoing senators and county councillors. Because they are all politicians, they usually vote for the candidates of their own party, so the Seanad reflects the strength of political parties. If that wasn't enough to keep the Seanad in the control of the government of the day, the Taoiseach nominates 11 senators – so it is very unusual for the government not to have a majority in the Seanad.

Graduates of Trinity College Dublin elect three senators, and graduates of the National University of Ireland (University College Dublin, University College Cork, NUI Galway and Maynooth University) elect another three. The university senators are usually not members of any political party.

TRINITY AND THE NATIONAL UNIVERSITY OF IRELAND (NUI)

Trinity and the NUI were the only universities in Ireland when the Seanad was being designed, but since then others have been added – Dublin City University, University of Limerick, Technological University Dublin and so on. But graduates from those universities don't get a vote. This may seem unfair – and even more unfair when you discover there was a referendum in 1979, more than 40 years ago, to allow the rules to be changed to give them a vote. The proposal was supported by 92 per cent of voters, but since then, no government has bothered to change the law. Some people are very cross about this. Not me, though – I have a vote because I went to UCD!

THE PRESIDENT

THE PRESIDENT OF IRELAND IS THE HEAD OF STATE AND, ACCORDING TO THE CONSTITUTION OF IRELAND, 'TAKES PRECEDENCE OVER ALL OTHER PERSONS IN THE STATE'. THE PRESIDENT LIVES IN ÁRAS AN UACHTARÁIN, A BIG HOUSE IN THE PHOENIX PARK IN DUBLIN. THEY ARE THE ONLY OFFICE-HOLDER DIRECTLY ELECTED BY ALL CITIZENS IN THE COUNTRY.

The President appoints the Taoiseach and the members of the government; summons the Dáil to meet; signs legislation into law; is the supreme commander of the defence forces; and has the right to pardon or reduce the sentences of people convicted by the courts.

Pretty powerful, right? Well – no, not really. In fact, the President has very little *real* power because all of the things listed above can only be done 'on the advice of' the Taoiseach or the government or the Dáil. The President appoints the Taoiseach nominated by the Dáil; appoints the ministers nominated by the Taoiseach and approved by the Dáil; and is *required* to sign laws passed by the Dáil or Seanad. Like a constitutional monarch, the President has a ceremonial role, putting the official seal of approval on decisions taken by others.

GUARDIAN OF THE CONSTITUTION

But there are *some* things the President can do that are important and could stop a government that was up to no good.

First of all, although the President is required to sign legislation passed by the Dáil and Seanad into law, they can decide to send it to the Supreme Court first to test whether or not it is in line with the Constitution (the rulebook for how the country is run). If the Supreme Court rules against the legislation – or part of it – it cannot become law. But if the Supreme Court decides that the legislation is constitutional, it can *never* be challenged in court again. This is one of the reasons this power isn't used very often.

Second, if a majority of senators, and at least one-third of TDs, ask that a particular law is put to a public vote, the President can decide to agree. This power has never been used.

Third, the President has to agree to a request from the Taoiseach to hold a general election – *unless* the Taoiseach no longer has the support of a majority of TDs. If that has happened, the President can refuse to allow a general election to go ahead. Although this power has never been used, it has been suggested several times as a way of avoiding an election and allowing the Dáil to choose a new government without asking the voters.

And that's about it. The President has an important symbolic role, representing the state and acting as guardian of the Constitution, but limited powers to do anything without the government's approval. In certain circumstances, those powers could be very important. They are a bit like an emergency charger for your phone: you rarely need it – but when you need it, you *really* need it!

PRESIDENTIAL AGE

Nobody under the age of 35 can be President. There was a referendum in 2015 on reducing the qualifying age to 21, but it was rejected by nearly three-quarters of those who voted. So you'll have to wait a while before aiming for the Áras …

LOCAL GOVERNMENT

AS WELL AS OUR NATIONAL OR CENTRAL GOVERNMENT, WE ALSO HAVE LOCAL GOVERNMENT, COUNCILS THAT RUN SERVICES IN COUNTIES AND SOME CITIES. THE CITIES OF DUBLIN, GALWAY AND CORK HAVE THEIR OWN COUNCILS; LIMERICK AND WATERFORD HAVE COUNCILS COVERING BOTH THE CITY AND THE COUNTY; AND THERE ARE 26 OTHER COUNTY COUNCILS. THE COUNTY OF DUBLIN IS SO LARGE AND DENSELY POPULATED THAT IT IS DIVIDED INTO THREE COUNCILS – FINGAL, DÚN LAOGHAIRE–RATHDOWN AND SOUTH COUNTY DUBLIN.

Councils look after lots of different things, including planning (deciding where houses or factories can be built), recreation (playgrounds and public swimming pools, for instance), libraries and firefighting services. They are also responsible for providing social housing for people who can't afford to buy or rent a home on their own.

But there are limits on what councils can do – most of their money comes from central government, so unless a council can get funding, it won't be able to do everything it wants. And if government ministers are providing money from their departments to pay for something, they usually like to take the credit for it themselves.

COUNCILLORS AND MAYORS

The politicians elected to serve on councils are called **COUNCILLORS**. There are 949 councillors in total, who are elected every five years. There are 63 on Dublin City Council, the largest, while several councils have just 18 members.

Each council elects a chairperson each year, called a cathaoirleach or mayor, or lord mayor in the case of Dublin and Cork. In 2019, the people of Cork, Limerick and Waterford were asked if they would like to have a directly elected mayor with more power, chosen by all the people rather than just by councillors. Only Limerick said yes. Discussions are continuing about having a directly elected mayor for Dublin, who would be in charge of all four councils in the capital.

A bit like the civil servants who run government departments, each local authority has its own staff, with a boss called the chief executive. Some of the functions of the council are carried out by the chief executive rather than the councillors.

OLD AND NEW

There is a lot of tradition associated with mayors because in most Irish cities the job dates back to the end of the 12th century. For instance, in Dublin the chain of office was made in 1698, and there is a Great Dublin Civic Sword, used during important ceremonies, that was made in the 1390s, and the Lord Mayor's carriage, which is used in the St Patrick's day parade, dates from 1791.

But not everything is so old – some mayors are themselves quite young. In June 2012, Darcy Lonergan became the youngest mayor in the country. She was elected Mayor of Carrickmacross town just a month before her 23rd birthday. But she didn't hold on to the record for long. In June 2016, Adam Wyse was elected Mayor of Waterford. He was just 22-and-1-month old! But as soon as you are 18, you can run for election as a councillor – so maybe you could try to beat the record!

WHERE DOES THE MONEY COME FROM?

AS WE'VE SEEN, THE GOVERNMENT PROVIDES MANY SERVICES THAT PEOPLE NEED AND EMPLOYS LOTS OF PEOPLE TO DELIVER THOSE SERVICES. RUNNING A COUNTRY COSTS A LOT, AND EACH YEAR THE GOVERNMENT ANNOUNCES THE BUDGET – THE PLAN FOR WHAT IT'S GOING TO SPEND DURING THE YEAR AND HOW IT INTENDS TO RAISE THE MONEY TO PAY FOR IT.

The Minister for Public Expenditure is in charge of how the money is spent. The Minister for Finance has the job of finding enough cash to balance the books. And the numbers are *big*. The Budget that was drawn up for 2020 (before the Covid-19 pandemic) had planned day-to-day spending of around 62 billion euro. That's €62,000,000,000.

HOW IS THE BUDGET SPENT?

The most expensive parts of the government to run are the three big-spending departments – Social Protection, Health and Education.

The Department of Social Protection helps people who are on low incomes for one reason or another, and it takes up about one-third of day-to-day spending. Among the people it helps are pensioners; people who are too ill to work; people who can't find a job; and families that don't earn very much and need some extra help from the government.

The next biggest chunk of the Budget goes on the Department of Health – think of all the nurses and doctors, all the hospitals and health centres, and you can see how expensive it is to run the health system. In the 2020 Budget – before Covid-19, remember – Health was due to get just under a quarter of all the money the government planned to spend.

Next is the Department of Education – there are a *lot* of teachers and SNAs who need to be paid, a lot of school buildings that need electricity and heat, and a lot of books to be bought for libraries, among many other things. The cost came in at around one-sixth of Budget 2020.

TAXES

So where does the government get its money? Mainly from taxes. People pay taxes on their **INCOME** – that's the money they earn from their job or business. The more you earn, the more you pay. Companies also have to pay tax on their profits. There are taxes on property, like your house, and on the car your family may own. And when you buy something in a shop, some of the money goes to the government as tax. As well as raising money to pay for running the country, taxes are sometimes used to discourage things that are bad for you – like smoking or drinking alcohol.

If the government can't raise enough to pay for everything it wants to do, it can borrow money. Lenders usually see Ireland as a good investment because it is relatively rich, stable and can be relied on to pay back the money it borrows.

At the time of writing, the National Debt – the amount of money the government owes to its lenders – was around €240 billion, or about €42,500 for every person in the state (that includes you!). And it was due to go up quite a bit because of the effects of Covid-19.

MINTED

In Ireland, our money is called the euro, a currency that is used in 19 member states of the European Union. Euro notes and coins were introduced on New Year's Day 2002, replacing the national currencies used up to then in each country. Each country makes its own coins and prints its own banknotes – ours are made in the Mint in Sandyford, County Dublin, a place with lots of security. The coins are the same on one side – showing a map of Europe – but each country has its own design on the other side. Irish euro coins have a harp on them. How many different countries can you find on the coins in your pocket?

HOW DO WE ELECT OUR LEADERS?

Life is full of choices to make. What jumper will I wear today? What will I have for breakfast? What book will I read? Obviously, you have chosen to read *this* book, which seems like a smart choice – well done!

Politics is all about choices too. Politicians have to make choices all day every day, choices that affect our lives in many different ways. We don't have to make choices about politics as often, but in a way our political choices are even more important because we choose the politicians who make the decisions on our behalf.

If we make good choices, we pick politicians who are able to do the job properly, who are able to co-operate for the good of the country, and who really care about what's best for all of us. If we make bad choices – well, then we're all in trouble. Different countries have different ways of choosing their politicians, and the system used is important. Does it help the voters to pick the most suitable politicians? Does it give everyone a fair chance – women as well as men, young candidates as well as old, ethnic minorities and people from different backgrounds? Do people trust it? Do they understand how it works?

There are arguments for and against every electoral system, and we'll look at some of them in this section. The most important thing is that, whatever system is used, it helps us to choose the best people to run the country.

WHAT IS AN ELECTION?

AN ELECTION IS A VOTE TO CHOOSE SOMEONE FOR A JOB. THAT MIGHT MEAN SELECTING A TD, OR THE PRESIDENT, OR THE CHAIRPERSON OF YOUR LOCAL GAA CLUB.

If more than one person wants a particular job, there has to be a way of choosing between them. Before an election can happen, a number of choices have to be made: who is allowed to vote, for instance, or where they can vote, or when the election should be. But the most important question is how do we decide who has won? In any race, you need to know where the finishing line is.

FIRST PAST THE POST

The simplest answer is to say that the person who gets the most votes wins the election. This is called **PLURALITY VOTING**, or first past the post. It is the system used in Britain and in the USA. The country is divided into constituencies, each of which has its own first-past-the-post election for a member of parliament or congress. It is simple and easy to understand – but is it fair? For example, say eleven people are trying to choose among three candidates to be their leader. Dan gets five votes, while Laura gets four and Seán gets two. Does Dan win because he got the most votes? That might seem fair, but on the other hand, six people preferred a different candidate – so a majority of voters did *not* choose Dan.

MAJORITY SYSTEM

What if there was a different system? What if a candidate had to get more than half the votes to win? In this case, Seán would be knocked out because he has the fewest votes, and the two people who voted for him would have to choose again, between Laura and Dan. If they both vote for Laura, then she will have six votes, giving her more than half the votes, and she will win. This is called a **MAJORITY SYSTEM**. In an election, this can be done by asking voters to rank the candidates in the order they prefer – so in this case, someone who said Seán was their favourite candidate by putting a number one against his name would put a number two beside the candidate they like second best. This is how our own system works when there is just one job to fill, like in a presidential election. Or you could have a second round of voting – the first round finds out who the two most popular candidates are, and then voters have to go back to vote again to choose between them. This is how elections are run in France.

PROPORTIONAL REPRESENTATION

Things can be done a little bit differently when there is more than one job to be filled – for instance, in a national parliament. Then another system can be used – **PROPORTIONAL REPRESENTATION (PR)**. This gives each party or group a share of the seats in the parliament that is more or less equal to their share of the vote – so a party that wins 30 per cent of the vote should get around 30 per cent of the seats.

MIXED SYSTEM

In other countries, there is a mixed system, where voters choose a representative from their constituency and also vote for a political party at the national or regional level. Half the seats in parliament are filled by the constituency representatives, and the rest are shared out to make sure each party gets a share of the seats equal to its share of the overall vote.

And then there is the Irish system, which we'll look at shortly. But which is best – proportional representation or first past the post?

PLURALITY: First past the post is decisive, straightforward and easy to understand, and it gives politicians a close connection to their voters.

The answer is clear under first past the post – and so is the choice, because you usually only have two big parties.

First past the post gives you strong government – and it is fair because the party with the most support, even if it doesn't have a majority, gets to hold power.

Coalition means compromise – so nobody is really getting the policies they voted for.

Your way could allow small parties with extreme views to hold the balance of power!

PR: But it can be very unfair – you can easily win a majority of the seats with a minority of the vote, so the votes of most of the people are wasted.

Under PR, lots of different parties can win seats, so there is a way for all views to be represented in parliament and in government.

But with PR a couple of different parties can come together and form a coalition, so the views of more voters are represented in government.

But a compromise will get you closer to the views of most of the voters.

Your way could allow a big party, without the support of most voters, to impose its policies on the rest of the country!

TOO CLOSE TO CALL

In an election, every vote can count. In the 2002 general election, Michael Finucane of Fine Gael lost his seat in the Limerick West constituency – he was beaten by his party colleague Dan Neville by just one vote. That's one vote out of a total of just over 40,000 cast in the constituency.

POLLING STATION
IONAD VÓTÁLA →

HOW WE VOTE IN IRELAND: PR-STV

HERE IN IRELAND, WE USE A SYSTEM CALLED PROPORTIONAL REPRESENTATION USING A SINGLE TRANSFERABLE VOTE (PR–STV).

This system is also used in Northern Ireland and Malta, and for some elections in Australia, New Zealand, India and Pakistan. Some people complain that this system is too complicated. But while the counting can be a bit difficult to follow, the actual voting is very easy. All you do is vote for the candidates in the order you like. In Ireland, we use a piece of paper, called a ballot paper, with the names of all the candidates printed on it. Voters mark their choices with a pencil. Some countries have voting machines instead of ballot papers, with voters pushing buttons to make their choice.

Some people only vote for their favourite candidate, giving them a number 1. Others vote for all the candidates of their favourite party, giving them a 1, 2 or 3. Others vote all the way down the list – so if there are 12 candidates in that constituency, they'll give their favourite candidate a number 1, then go all the way down to the one they like least, giving them a number 12.

If a voter makes a mistake by not clearly indicating who they want to vote for, the vote is **SPOILED** and isn't counted. Some people spoil their vote deliberately because they don't like any of the candidates. But how you fill out your ballot paper is entirely up to you – and only you know how you voted, because you vote in secret: nobody else gets to see how you filled out your ballot paper.

QUOTAS

So what happens once you've made your choice? Remember we talked about the finishing line – how you know who's won the race? Under PR-STV, the finishing line is the **QUOTA** – the number of votes a candidate needs to win a seat. All the votes from the constituency are brought to the count centre and sorted. Any spoiled votes are put aside, and all the valid votes are counted. Once you know how many valid votes there are, you can work out the quota – the number of votes needed to win a seat.

There is a maths formula to work this out, but it's very simple: the total number of valid votes, divided by the number of seats plus one, with one added. This gives the lowest number of votes that will fill all the seats, but *only* the number of seats available. Say it is a four-seat constituency, and there are 10,000 valid votes. You divide 10,000 by the number of seats plus one, which is five. This gives you 2,000, and you then add one – so the quota is 2,001. If four candidates have 2,001 votes, there are only 1,996 votes left – so you fill four seats, but *only* four seats.

It would be very easy if all the seats were filled on the first count – but it wouldn't be nearly as exciting! One or two of the candidates might have more votes than the quota on the first count, but often there are none. This is where transfers come in.

TRANSFERS

Remember your ballot paper where you gave your **PREFERENCES** – giving a number to the candidates in the order you liked them? Well, those preferences come into play if your vote is **TRANSFERRED** – it is given to the next candidate in the order you chose. So if your number one choice is gone, it is given to the candidate you marked with a 2, and so on down the list. Transfers come about in two ways. First, there may be a **SURPLUS**. If a candidate is elected and they have more votes than the quota, those extra votes are taken away and distributed. The second way transfers happen is if seats still need to be filled after all surplus votes have been transferred. Then the candidate with the lowest number of votes is **ELIMINATED**, and their votes are given to the next highest candidate on each ballot paper.

And this continues until all the seats are filled. At the end, some candidates might be elected without reaching the quota. Because some people won't have given their preferences all the way down the ballot paper, their votes can't be transferred and so become **NON-TRANSFERABLE**. Once all the votes that can be transferred have been shared out, if there are still two candidates in the running for the last seat, the one with most votes wins, even if they don't reach the quota.

SEE IT IN ACTION!

Probably the best way to understand PR-STV is to see it in action – so here's an example.

Say we have 38,000 valid votes and three seats to be filled. We use our formula – valid votes divided by the number of seats plus one, plus one – to work out the quota, which is 9,501. On the first count, the Blue Party candidate is elected because they have more votes than the quota, and a surplus of 1,999 votes. When the surplus votes are shared out according to second preferences (given to those who are number 2 on the surplus votes), no other candidate reaches the quota, so the Purple Party candidate is eliminated. When their 3,069 votes are shared out, a lot of them go to the Orange Party candidate, taking them ahead of the Pink Party, who is then eliminated. Those votes elect the Red Party candidate, who has a surplus. Now there is only one seat left, with two candidates still in the running. The Yellow candidate is just 150 votes ahead of Orange. It all comes down to the transfer of Red's surplus. Orange does much better than Yellow and is elected without reaching the quota.

So that is PR-STV – not as complicated as it looks, is it? And if you understand it, you are doing better than quite a few adults!

VALID VOTES: 38,000   SEATS: 3   QUOTA: 9,501

Candidate	First Count		Second Count		Third Count		Fourth Count		
Blue	11,500 ELECTED!	−1,999							
Red	8,000	+900	8,900	+500	9,400	+2,000	11,400 ELECTED!	−1,899	
Yellow	6,000	+550	6,550	+200	6,750	+1,500	8,250	+600	8,850 ELIMINATED!
Pink	5,500	+300	5,800	+100	5,900 ELIMINATED!	−5,900			
Orange	4,000	+100	4,100	+2,000	6,100	+2,000	8,100	+900	9,000 ELECTED!
Purple	3,000	+69	3,069 ELIMINATED!	−3,069					
NON-TRANSFERABLE		80		269		400		399	

WHO CAN VOTE?

WHO GETS TO VOTE? IN ORDER TO VOTE IN IRELAND, YOU HAVE TO BE OVER 18, YOU HAVE TO BE LIVING IN THE STATE AND YOU HAVE TO BE REGISTERED, WHICH MEANS FILLING OUT A FORM TO MAKE SURE YOU'RE ON THE LIST OF VOTERS.

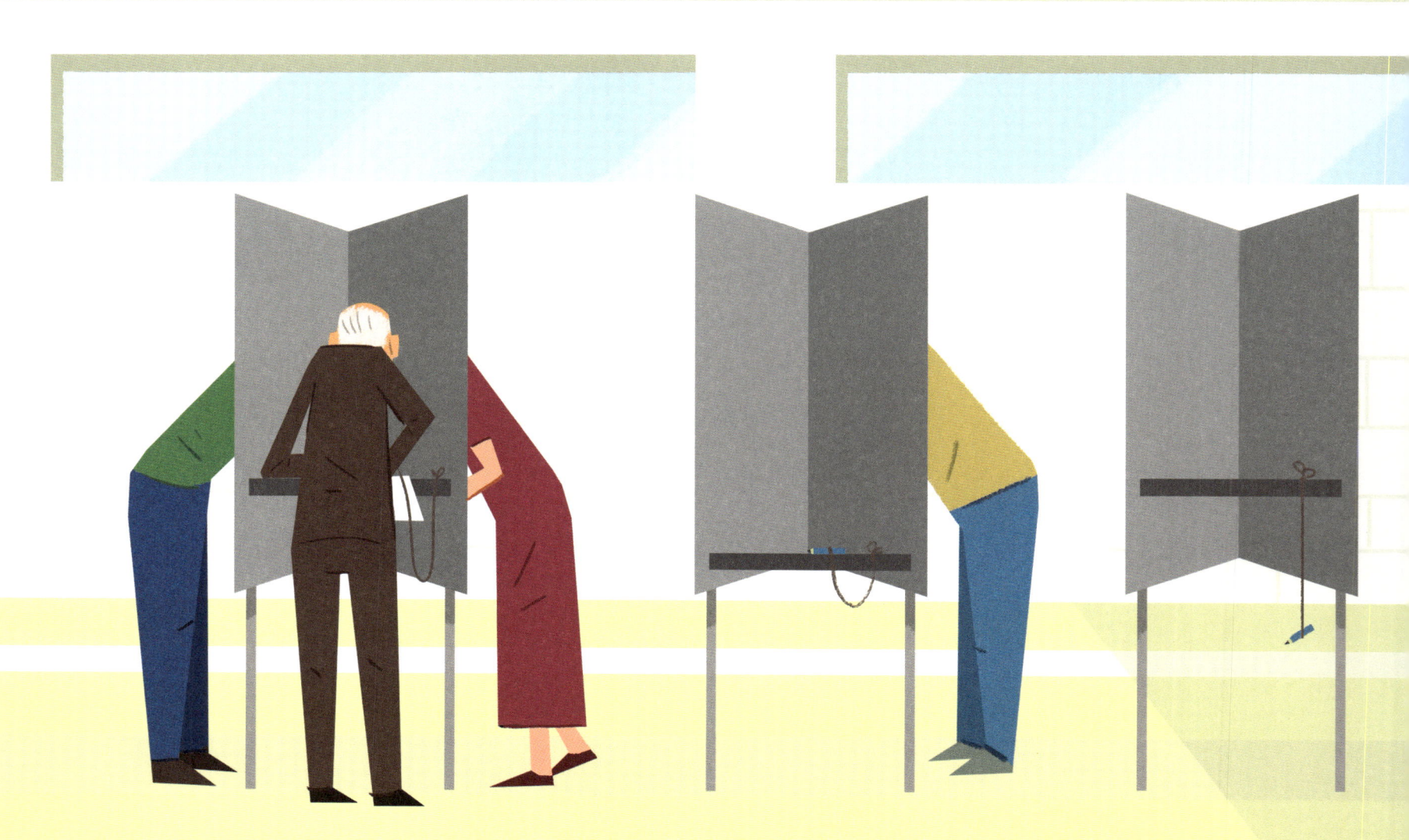

There are plenty of opportunities to vote. There is a general election – voting for the Dáil – at least every five years, sometimes more often if a government is defeated on an important vote, or if the Taoiseach of the day thinks there is a political advantage in having an early election. There are local elections – for councils – every five years, at the same time as elections to the European Parliament. There is a presidential election every seven years. And then there are constitutional referendums fairly regularly as well.

People who live here but who aren't citizens of an EU country are only allowed to vote in local elections. EU citizens can vote in local and European elections. British citizens can vote in Dáil, European and local elections. Only Irish citizens can vote in presidential elections and referendums, as well as Dáil, European and local elections.

Two suggestions are being talked about that would allow more people to vote.

THE VOTING AGE

The first is to lower the voting age from 18 to 16. Some people argue that 16- and 17-year-olds aren't grown up enough to take part in elections and wouldn't be interested anyway. On the other hand, if they were allowed to vote, they might take more interest – and in any case, decisions taken by politicians today will affect them for longer than anyone else. What do you think?

THE IRISH ABROAD

The second is to give Irish citizens who don't live in Ireland the right to vote in some elections. Many countries allow citizens living abroad to vote – including the United States and France. This allows people who have left those countries to stay involved in their political life, so they keep a connection with their home country.

But some people see problems with this, especially for a country like Ireland that has seen lots of emigration and that allows people who have never lived here to become citizens if they have Irish ancestors. For example, what would happen if citizens abroad were allowed to vote in a general election and elected a government that wanted to increase taxes on people who live in Ireland? Would that be fair to people living here?

Maybe not – but what about giving citizens abroad the right to vote without affecting the government of the country? That's why there is a suggestion that Irish citizens abroad should be allowed to take part in the election of the President – a mainly symbolic office.

COMPULSORY VOTING

Twenty-two countries around the world have *compulsory voting* – unless you have a good excuse, you could be fined or even jailed if you don't take part in an election. Many South American countries have mandatory voting, as do Australia and, in the EU, Belgium, Bulgaria, Greece and Luxembourg. The dictatorship of North Korea also requires its citizens to vote – even though there is only ever one candidate on the ballot paper!

HOW DO WE KEEP THE RULES?

If you want to play a game, you have to know what the rules are – and agree to follow them.

If someone suggests a game of football, you have to know whether you're playing Gaelic, soccer or rugby – otherwise it could get very messy very quickly. The same applies to society. If we're all going to get along with each other, we need to know that there are rules that are followed, and that if someone breaks those rules there will be consequences. For instance, stealing is against the law, and if someone steals your bike, it's good to know that they'll get in trouble if they're caught (and you'll hopefully get your bike back).

The rules we have to follow in society are called **LAWS**, which are passed by the Oireachtas and which everyone is supposed to follow in the same way. Nobody can claim a law doesn't apply to them because of who they are – according to the Constitution, everybody should be treated as **EQUAL BEFORE THE LAW**.

Most people keep within the law – mainly because it's the right thing to do, but partly because they don't want to get into trouble. If people do break the law, they may find themselves answering awkward questions from the Gardaí, and perhaps end up in court. On balance, it's probably best to keep to the rules.

THE CONSTITUTION

THE RULEBOOK FOR HOW SOCIETY IS RUN IS CALLED THE CONSTITUTION – IT IS THE BASIC LAW SETTING OUT HOW THE SYSTEM OF GOVERNMENT WORKS.

Our Constitution – called in Irish Bunreacht na hÉireann – came into force after it was approved by a majority of voters in 1937.

It says that the power to rule Ireland comes from the Irish people themselves and sets out our system of government as a 'sovereign, independent, democratic state', with a president, a parliament made up of the Dáil and the Seanad, a government led by a taoiseach, and a system of justice carried out by the courts.

RIGHTS

It also outlines the fundamental rights of citizens. For instance, it says that citizens can only be arrested or put in prison according to the law. This means that the government can't just lock up anyone they don't like – the person has to have broken a law. In the same way, the Constitution says nobody can enter your house if there isn't a law that says they can. Among other things, citizens have the right to free speech, to own property and to practise their religion.

'THE COMMON GOOD'

But these rights don't come without some limits, because the people who wrote the Constitution knew that sometimes the rights of individuals need to be balanced against the good of society as a whole. For instance, the Constitution says there is a right to own property – but it also says that this right ought to be regulated by 'the principles of social justice' and the 'common good'.

So an argument might be made that, in the middle of a housing crisis, your right to own something – say a house that you don't live in – is less important than the need to find people somewhere to live. This might mean that the government would be able to give the empty house to a homeless family.

Other rights, like the right to free speech or to practise your religion, are 'subject to public order and morality'. You have the right to worship the sun if you want to. But what if you want to do that by going to the centre of Dublin at noon, taking off all your clothes and dancing to celebrate the sun reaching the highest point in the sky? That would make for an interesting conversation with a Garda!

CREATE YOUR OWN CONSTITUTION

If you were writing a constitution, what would you include? What rights would you give to people, and how would you set the rules for how decisions are made? You can give it a go – why not write a constitution for how your class or your home is run? Start by defining exactly who is a member of the group and what important values you share. Set out the rights and duties of the people in the group – who does the jobs that need to be done, and how do you make sure everyone is treated fairly? Explain how decisions are made and how disagreements are resolved. Hopefully, when the rules are written down everyone will find it easier to get along!

REFERENDUMS

IMAGINE A SOCCER MATCH WHERE ONE TEAM COULD CHANGE THE RULES OF THE GAME ANY TIME THEY WANTED. THEY MIGHT DECIDE TO REMOVE THEIR GOAL SO THE OTHER SIDE COULDN'T SCORE. GUESS WHO WOULD WIN THE GAME!

Some rules are so important that they should be difficult to change – like the Constitution. Ordinary laws can be changed by a majority in the Dáil and Seanad, but not the Constitution, because it's the fundamental rulebook for the state. If a government could change it whenever it wanted, it might bend the rules so it could stay in power for ever – a bit like the soccer team with no goal.

But while changing the Constitution can't be too easy, it has to be possible if really necessary. Society has changed a lot since the Constitution was written in the 1930s, and as a result it needs some rewriting every now and then.

CONSTITUTIONAL REFERENDUMS

So, unlike ordinary laws, which are decided on by the Dáil and Seanad, a change to Bunreacht na hÉireann has to be approved by a majority of voters. This is called a **CONSTITUTIONAL REFERENDUM**.

The proposed change, or amendment, to the Constitution must first be passed by the Dáil and Seanad. Then voters get to have their say. It's a simple yes or no question, so it's much easier to count than an election under PR-STV.

Since the Constitution was approved in 1937, there have been 39 referendums on proposed amendments (sometimes more than one referendum is held on the same day). Of those, 11 have been rejected and 28 accepted.

Some amendments are about the political system. Two attempts to get rid of PR-STV, in 1959 and 1968, were rejected by the voters. In 1972, the voting age was lowered from 21 to 18; while in 2015, a proposal to allow people younger than 35 to stand for the presidency was defeated. An attempt to get rid of the Seanad was defeated in 2013.

There have been lots of referendums about the European Union. In 1971, 83 per cent voted in favour of joining the EU. Since then, every time there was a change to the rules of how the EU is run, we've had a vote on it. Twice – in 2001 and 2008 – Irish voters rejected a new treaty on how Europe works, but on both occasions some changes were made and the treaties were accepted in a second vote.

Among the other amendments passed in recent years were changes recognising the Good Friday Agreement, which brought peace to Northern Ireland (1998), abolishing the death penalty (2001), and allowing same-sex couples to get married (2015).

SCHOOL REFERENDUM

If you could change one thing in your school, what would it be? Would you like a longer break time – say an extra 10 minutes, with the time added on at the end of the day? Some people might like that, but others might prefer to keep things as they are so they continue to get home a bit earlier. The best way to find out what people think is to ask them. Maybe your principal would let you hold a referendum about it – and then you might end up with an extra 10 minutes to enjoy yourself at break time!

SEPARATION OF POWERS

WE GIVE THE GOVERNMENT A LOT OF POWER OVER OUR LIVES, AND THE GOVERNMENT MAKES SURE WE FOLLOW THE RULES. BUT HOW CAN WE MAKE SURE THAT THE GOVERNMENT ITSELF FOLLOWS THE RULES AND DOESN'T TREAT PEOPLE UNFAIRLY?

One way is to divide power, so that different parts of the government keep an eye on each other, and no one part can do what it wants without limits. This is the idea behind the separation of powers between three branches of government: the legislative, executive and judicial. The legislature (also known as parliament) **MAKES** the laws; the executive (also called the government) **IMPLEMENTS** the laws; the judiciary (or the courts, as they are also called) **INTERPRETS** the laws.

HOW DOES IT WORK?

Let's look at an example. Imagine the government wants to raise some extra money by introducing a tax – let's say it wants to make everyone who owns a skateboard pay a special €10 skateboard tax. First, it has to get the legislature – the parliament – to pass a law introducing the tax. Now, there may be skateboarding politicians who would argue against the tax, but probably not that many, so let's assume the law is passed. Skateboarders wouldn't be very happy, would they? They might say the tax is unfair because cyclists don't have to pay it, and they could take a case to the courts, asking the judges to decide if the tax is within the rules. The judges would hear arguments from both sides and might decide that the tax was unfair – so the skateboarders would save €10 each, and the government would have to think up a new way to raise the money.

The separation of powers is most obvious in a presidential system like in the United States, where the executive (the President) is distinct from the legislature (the Congress). It's a bit less obvious in a parliamentary system like ours, where the executive (the government, led by the Taoiseach) is made up of members of the legislature (the Dáil and Seanad). But the idea of dividing power remains – the government needs the support of the Dáil to get things done, and if it loses that support, then it has to resign. And the judiciary keeps an eye on what they are both up to, making sure that what they are doing is fair and within the rules of the Constitution.

Another way of thinking about it is to imagine that there was no separation of powers – that the government of the day controlled both the parliament and the judiciary. It could pass whatever laws it liked, and nobody could go to court to challenge what it did. The government would have total control, and there would be no way of stopping it doing something unfair.

TALK TALK TALK

Another word for legislature is 'parliament' – this comes from the French word *parler*, which means 'to speak'. And politicians do like to speak – a lot! In Ireland, the parliament is called the Oireachtas, made up of the Dáil and the Seanad.

THE LEGISLATURE

THE EXECUTIVE

THE JUDICIARY

THE COURTS

THE COURTS ARE WHERE LEGAL CASES ARE DECIDED. THERE ARE DIFFERENT LEVELS OF COURT TO DEAL WITH DIFFERENT TYPES OF CASES. THE LEAST SERIOUS ARE DECIDED IN THE DISTRICT COURT. MORE IMPORTANT ONES ARE DEALT WITH IN THE CIRCUIT COURT. AND THE MOST SERIOUS COME BEFORE THE HIGH COURT. THE SUPREME COURT IS AT THE TOP OF THE SYSTEM. IT HEARS APPEALS AGAINST DECISIONS BY THE LOWER COURTS.

CRIMINAL AND CIVIL

There are two types of court cases – criminal and civil. If it is a **CRIMINAL** matter, the state prosecutes someone (takes them to court) for committing a crime – theft, or assault, or road traffic offences. If found guilty, the accused could be sent to prison or fined.

CIVIL cases, on the other hand, are where one person is in a dispute with another individual or an organisation. For instance, you could be looking for money from someone who has damaged your property or from an employer who has treated you unfairly, or there could be a court case about which parent should look after the children after a marriage breaks up.

Say, for example, a man driving a car knocks you off your bike. If the Gardaí think he was driving dangerously, they might decide to prosecute him – this would be a criminal case, and if found guilty he could end up in jail. That might make you feel a *bit* better, but you might decide that you'd feel a *lot* better if you were paid money to make up for what happened. This is called **COMPENSATION**. So you might look to sue the driver for compensation. This would be a civil case, and it could result in the driver paying you money to make up for the injuries he caused you.

CHILDREN

Sometimes, children can be taken to court, but they are not treated the same way as adults, and there are age limits. For most offences, children can only be brought to court if they are aged 12 or over, though for some very serious crimes children as young as 10 can be prosecuted. If found guilty, children aged between 10 and 17 might be sent to a children's detention facility, but nobody can be sent to prison until they are at least 18.

There is a special children's court where these cases are heard, and there are strict rules preventing the identification of any child accused of a crime – their name or photograph can't be published in the newspapers or shown on television news.

PRISON

As we've seen, people who are found guilty of crimes are sometimes sent to jail (also called prison). Why is this? Some people say that if someone has done something bad, they should be punished; that they can't commit any other crimes while they are in prison; and that locking people up is a warning to others of what might happen to them if they break the law.

But some argue that prison is pointless and that locking people up does nothing to make them better citizens. It is no guarantee that they won't commit more crimes when they are let out. They argue for alternatives, like **RESTORATIVE JUSTICE**, which tries to reconcile the offender with their victims and the wider community. For example, the offender might apologise to the victim and then do community work to make up for their bad behaviour. What do you think?

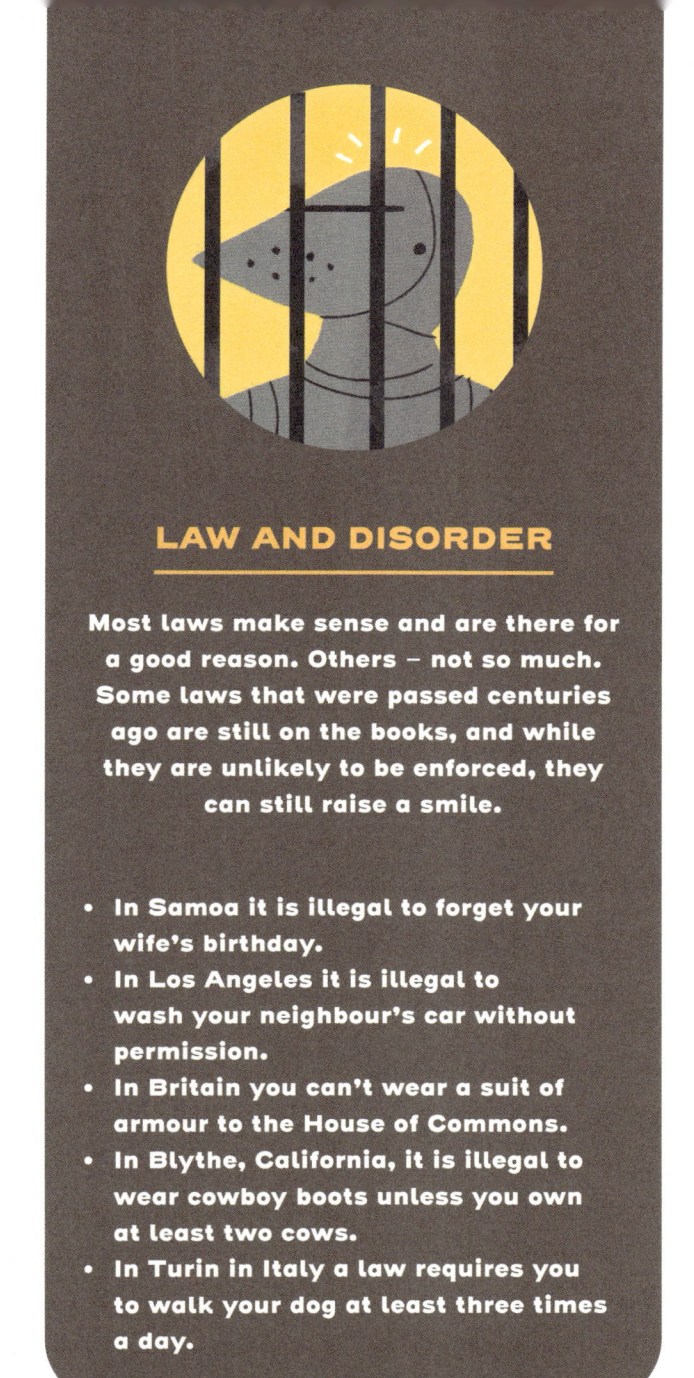

LAW AND DISORDER

Most laws make sense and are there for a good reason. Others – not so much. Some laws that were passed centuries ago are still on the books, and while they are unlikely to be enforced, they can still raise a smile.

- In Samoa it is illegal to forget your wife's birthday.
- In Los Angeles it is illegal to wash your neighbour's car without permission.
- In Britain you can't wear a suit of armour to the House of Commons.
- In Blythe, California, it is illegal to wear cowboy boots unless you own at least two cows.
- In Turin in Italy a law requires you to walk your dog at least three times a day.

THE FOUR COURTS >

AN GARDA SÍOCHÁNA

THE POLICE FORCE IN IRELAND IS CALLED AN GARDA SÍOCHÁNA, WHICH MEANS 'GUARDIANS OF THE PEACE'. GENERALLY, ONE MEMBER OF THE FORCE IS CALLED A GARDA OR A GUARD; SEVERAL MEMBERS ARE CALLED GARDAÍ OR GUARDS.

There are around 14,000 Gardaí, based at stations around the country. There is no longer a minimum height requirement, but applicants have to pass a fitness test. They must be over 18, but under 35 years old, and they have to be able to use two languages, one of which must be English or Irish.

WHO CAN BECOME A GARDA?

Citizens of Ireland or the EU are allowed to become Gardaí. So are recognised refugees and people who have lived legally in the state for a full year and for four of the previous eight years before applying. Initial training takes place at the Garda College in Templemore, County Tipperary, for eight months, followed by another eight months' on-the-job training in a Garda station.

There is also a Garda Reserve of unpaid volunteers who help the main force. Members are trained at the Garda College and have some Garda powers while on duty, but they are supervised by regular Garda members. People between the ages of 18 and 60 are eligible to join the Garda Reserve.

WHAT DO THE GARDAÍ DO?

An Garda Síochána says that its mission is 'Keeping People Safe' – so how do they do this? The Gardaí have the power to stop you if they suspect you are breaking certain laws. They have the power to search you if they have a reasonable suspicion that you have broken the law. They have the power to enter your home if they are pursuing a suspect or if they have permission from a judge (called a 'search warrant'). And they can arrest you, which means they take you to the Garda station and you are not allowed to leave.

But, in anything they do, Gardaí have to act in line with the Constitution and with the European Convention on Human Rights, as well as with various court rulings. If they fail to do so, they may be acting unlawfully and could get in trouble themselves. And they have to take extra care to respect the rights of anyone under the age of 18. If someone under the age of 18 is arrested, their parents or guardians have to be told, and they can't be questioned unless their parent or guardian is there.

A GARDA'S BEST FRIEND

With their great sense of smell, dogs can be a big help in police work, sniffing out evidence, drugs or explosives and helping to find missing people.

The Garda Dog Unit uses different breeds for different jobs. German Shepherds are great at tracking people, while Labradors and Springer Spaniels can sniff out illegal drugs or explosives.

It takes three or four weeks of assessment to see if dogs are suitable, then at least another eight weeks to train them to search. Each dog has its own handler and lives with them so they can build up a close relationship – though the dogs understand the difference between working and being off-duty.

THE DEFENCE FORCES

THE DEFENCE FORCES ARE THE ARMED FORCES OF THE STATE, MADE UP OF THE ARMY, AIR CORPS AND NAVAL SERVICE.

The Defence Forces trace their history back to the formation of the Irish Volunteers in 1913. The Volunteers were central to the 1916 Easter Rising and the War of Independence that followed. The name of the Defence Forces in Irish – Óglaigh na hÉireann – is taken from the Volunteers, as is the cap badge still worn by members.

The mission of the Defence Forces is to defend the country against attack, to help the Gardaí and other state services when asked, and to take part in peacekeeping missions abroad.

The Defence Forces also have an important ceremonial role, taking part in commemorations and state events, including funerals. Troops might provide a guard of honour, or march in a parade, or fire salutes with rifles or artillery, or provide music with an Army band.

DIVISIONS OF THE DEFENCE FORCES

The Army is the largest part of the Defence Forces. It is responsible for operations on land – anything not at sea or in the air. It has two brigades. The 1st Brigade covers the south of the country while the 2nd Brigade looks after the northern half of the state. Each brigade has a range of specialised troops – the infantry, or foot soldiers; the artillery, which operates large guns; the cavalry, which uses armoured cars and tanks; and engineers, who use their skills to make sure the Defence Forces can live, move and operate wherever they are – engineers might have to build bridges, remove obstacles or dismantle bombs. Each brigade also has transport and medical personnel. The Defence Forces Training Centre is based in the Curragh in County Kildare.

The Army Ranger Wing is the special operations force of the Defence Forces. Rangers are highly trained and extremely fit. The Ranger Wing has a role in dealing with terrorist threats, and in wartime it would operate behind enemy lines.

The Air Corps has a range of helicopters and fixed-wing aircraft. Its main job is to defend Irish airspace and to support Army operations. But it also does lots of other things – flying sick people to hospital, delivering supplies to islands and other isolated areas cut off by bad weather, helping in search and rescue missions, keeping an eye on what is happening at sea, and flying ministers to meetings abroad.

The Naval Service defends the sea around Ireland. It makes sure fishing boats are operating within the law and arrests those that aren't, as well as looking for ships trying to smuggle drugs or people through Irish waters. The Naval Service has eight ships.

As well as the full-time Permanent Defence Forces, there is also an Army Reserve – volunteers who take part in Army training in their spare time. Reservists usually do a minimum of seven days of paid full-time training a year, as well as at least 48 hours of voluntary service.

There are two ways of joining the Army – as a recruit, or ordinary soldier, or as an officer cadet. To join the Army, you must be between 18 and 25 and have to pass physical fitness tests. It takes 17 weeks to train a recruit and 17 months to train an officer cadet.

FIT FOR ACTION

To be a soldier, you need to be *fit*. In order to qualify as a possible recruit, you have to be able to:

- Do 20 push-ups in 1 minute
- Do 20 sit-ups in 1 minute
- Run 2.4 kilometres in 11 minutes 40 seconds for men, and 13 minutes 10 seconds for women

And you have to do the push-ups and sit-ups properly – if you don't, they won't count!

THE MEDIA

BEFORE YOU DECIDE WHAT YOU THINK ABOUT AN ISSUE, OR HOW YOU SHOULD VOTE IN AN ELECTION, YOU NEED TO BE INFORMED. YOU NEED TO KNOW WHAT IS GOING ON, WHAT QUESTIONS NEED TO BE DECIDED IN ELECTIONS, WHAT THE VARIOUS PARTIES STAND FOR AND HOW DIFFERENT POLITICIANS WILL AFFECT YOUR LIFE IF THEY GET INTO POWER.

So how do you find out? Even in a small country like Ireland, it's not possible for every voter to know all their politicians. And busy people can't be expected to follow every twist and turn of what goes on in the Dáil or the details of all proposed legislation.

This is where the **MEDIA** come in. The media are the systems of communicating information to large numbers of people – such as television, radio, newspapers and the internet.

Most people rely on the media to find out what's going on – also known as **THE NEWS** or **CURRENT AFFAIRS**. They might read a newspaper, or watch the television news, or listen to a radio programme, or keep up with news on the internet by looking at websites or following social media feeds.

The media play an important role in politics by keeping citizens informed. They can also ask politicians questions the public would like answered. Seeing how politicians answer these questions gives people an idea of what they are like. And hearing policies being challenged lets voters decide whether they are sensible or not. Finally, the media can find out and make known things that the government or other organisations might want to keep quiet – like mistakes they have made.

CODE OF PRACTICE

There are rules to try to make sure that the media treat people fairly.

Newspapers have a code of practice that calls on them to be truthful, accurate, fair and honest in their coverage. They are allowed to express their views – strongly – *but* they must make it clear that it is only their opinion and they can't present it as fact.

Broadcasters are obliged by law to be **OBJECTIVE** (dealing with facts, despite any personal views), **IMPARTIAL** (not supporting one side over the other) and **FAIR**, and to avoid expressing their own view on an issue.

If somebody thinks they have been treated unfairly, they can complain – in the case of newspapers to the Press Council of Ireland, and for TV or radio stations to the Broadcasting Authority of Ireland. If that doesn't work, they can go to court to try to get the statement withdrawn, and perhaps to win money in compensation if their reputation is damaged. On page 66, we'll take a look at freedom of speech and the limits that are sometimes put on it.

Social media is not as well regulated as TV news, radio and newspapers, so sometimes false information can appear, designed to mislead people. When you see something online, it is worth taking a moment to ask whether it comes from a trustworthy source. If the information seems surprising and hasn't been published elsewhere, it may be because it isn't true.

Probably the safest course is to follow news from reliable sources, – broadcasters, newspapers or websites that are properly regulated. But try to get your information from a wide variety of outlets, so you get a fuller picture of what is really going on.

I READ THE NEWS TODAY, OH BOY ...

According to the Reuters Digital News Report 2021, the top online news sources in Ireland are RTÉ News online (rte.ie/news), TheJournal.ie; and Irish Independent online (independent.ie). All of these sites carry lots of news stories, but many of them are not designed to appeal to children.

RTÉ has a children's news programme, *news2day*, which is broadcast on RTÉ2 at 4.20 p.m. during term time – this covers the main news stories in a way that connects with its audience of 8- to 12-year-olds.

WHY CAN'T WE AGREE?

Disagreements are part of life — and they are certainly part of politics. But political disagreements tend to last longer and be fiercer than a disagreement you might have with your friends or your sister or brother. A row over what television programme to watch will get settled eventually — although if you take too long about it the show might be over!

But if the disagreement is about something more important — like how to pay for health care, for instance — then finding common ground between different ideas is trickier. People have strong views, based on their beliefs about how society should be organised, and they are reluctant to change their minds.

This doesn't make them bad people, and it doesn't mean they don't want the best for everyone. Someone might disagree with you about what to do, but their intentions can still be just as good as yours — they just think there is a better way to do it.

Another thing worth bearing in mind about political disagreements is that they are about complicated problems which are difficult to solve and may not have a perfect solution. They may not even have a *good* solution — just one that is less bad than the alternatives.

When someone seems to have an easy answer to a complicated problem, it's worth remembering what the American writer H.L. Mencken had to say: 'For every complex problem there is an answer that is clear, simple and wrong.'

So as we look at political differences, let's try not to fall out.

POLITICAL PARTIES

IF YOU LOOK THROUGH OUR CONSTITUTION – WHICH SETS OUT THE RULES OF HOW POLITICS WORKS – YOU'LL FIND NO MENTION OF ONE OF THE MOST IMPORTANT THINGS IN THE SYSTEM: POLITICAL PARTIES.

Parties are groups of people with similar views on major issues. Because they have a lot in common – whether they want more taxation to pay for government spending, or want to reduce spending so taxes can be cut, or whether they are rural or urban, or share a particular view on the environment – they tend to agree on lots of things.

Sometimes people vote for a party because it's a family tradition, and even if the party changes its position on a big issue, they'll keep voting for it.

In countries with a first-past-the-post system, like Britain and the United States, there are usually two main parties, one of which generally gets a majority and can govern on its own. In countries with proportional representation, there tend to be more than two main parties, and governments are normally **COALITIONS**, which means two or more parties joining together to form a government.

The main parties in Ireland are Sinn Féin, Fianna Fáil, Fine Gael, the Green Party, Labour, the Social Democrats and Solidarity/People Before Profit.

INDEPENDENTS

Ireland also has lots of independents – people who aren't a member of any party. In theory, all of the TDs elected to the Dáil could be independent, deciding on their own how they'll vote on each issue as it comes up.

In practice, that might be difficult. A government can only survive as long as a majority in the Dáil support it. If it isn't sure that it can get a majority, it could find it impossible to run the country.

THE PARTY LINE

Most members of the Dáil are members of parties, and they agree to vote the way the majority of the party decides. Each party has a member with the job of **WHIP**, who makes sure everyone votes the right way. If a TD decides they can't go along with the rest of the party in a vote, they will **LOSE THE WHIP** and will have to leave the party. The term 'whip' comes from foxhunting. The 'whipper-in' was the person who whipped all the hunting hounds into a pack, pointed them after the fox and ensured they didn't stray. The word began to be used in politics in England in the 18th century.

Parties help their members get elected – they tend to have more money to spend than independents, and they and their leaders get publicity in the national media, which can help candidates in their constituencies. In a general election, many people vote for the candidates of a particular party because they like its policies or its leader and want to see it in government.

JOKING AROUND

Politics is a serious business – most of the time. But many countries have had joke parties that ran in elections as a way of making fun of 'real' politicians.

In Serbia, a group of comedians formed a party called You Haven't Tasted the Sarma (sarma is stuffed cabbage, a traditional Serbian recipe). Its candidate came third in the 2017 presidential election, with nearly 10 per cent of the vote.

In Britain, the Official Monster Raving Loony Party has unsuccessfully taken part in elections for many years. Among its policies are reducing school class sizes by making kids sit closer together at smaller desks, and increasing the red squirrel population by painting half the grey squirrels red.

When democracy came to the former communist countries of Eastern Europe, lots of new parties sprang up – including joke beer-lovers' parties in Belarus, Russia and the Czech Republic. They didn't do too well, but their colleagues in Poland did, winning 3 per cent of the vote and 16 seats in parliament in 1991. But the joke didn't last – the party soon split, and some of its former members started taking politics seriously.

Canada's Rhinoceros Party promised to repeal the law of gravity, promote higher education by building taller schools and end crime by abolishing all laws. But it also promised that it wouldn't keep its election promises if its candidates were ever elected to anything (they weren't).

POLITICAL IDEOLOGIES

OFTEN PEOPLE SUPPORT A PARTICULAR POLITICAL PARTY BECAUSE THEY HAVE A SIMILAR IDEOLOGY – A SET OF IDEAS OR BELIEFS ABOUT HOW SOCIETY SHOULD BE ORGANISED.

Around the world, politicians and parties are often described as either 'left wing' or 'right wing'. What is the difference between them?

RIGHT VERSUS LEFT

Those on the right believe that the most important thing in society is to give each individual as much freedom as possible. They think the government should have less power so people can make their own decisions. They want taxes to be low so people can decide themselves how to spend their money. And they believe that businesses, rather than the government, should supply as many services as possible because that is the most efficient way of doing things.

Those on the left, on the other hand, are more interested in equality. They think the government should have more power so it can protect people in society who are less well off. They think people with more money should pay more in tax to pay for government services for everyone. And they think those services should be provided free, so that being able to pay for a service doesn't give you an unfair advantage.

If you were very right wing, you would believe in a very restricted role for government – it would only be involved in defending the country and enforcing basic laws. If you were very left wing, you would believe the government should control nearly everything and decide what resources each member of society should get. But, of course, most people aren't at either extreme – they are somewhere in the middle.

Left versus right isn't the only difference between parties. Sometimes there are parties that represent farmers, as opposed to parties based in the cities. Or there might be divisions between parties over religion. There are also parties who think the most important thing is saving the environment.

FIANNA FÁIL VERSUS FINE GAEL

Here in Ireland, for most of the last century, the two main parties were Fianna Fáil and Fine Gael. The division between them wasn't really about left and right – both were pretty much in the middle, and could become a bit more left or a bit more right wing if it suited. Their differences began over the treaty with Britain that gave Ireland independence. Fianna Fáil descended from those who argued the treaty didn't give enough freedom, while Fine Gael's origins were in the group that said it was the best deal available.

In 2020, for the first time, Fianna Fáil and Fine Gael went into government together, nearly 100 years after the split over the treaty. The Green Party was also part of the coalition.

This left Sinn Féin, a more left-wing party, as the biggest opposition party. Also in opposition were the left-of-centre Labour and Social Democrats parties, and the more left-wing Solidarity/People Before Profit, as well as a large number of independents.

RIGHT-WINGER: If taxes are low, and people can keep more of what they earn, they'll work harder. This will create more wealth, and society will be better off.

LEFT-WINGER: People need the government to give them a helping hand if they're out of work or sick. There needs to be a safety net so they don't suffer, and people should pay for that through taxes. And the more you earn, the more you can afford to pay.

But that just discourages people from working hard! And that means less money to pay for things like schools and hospitals.

If the rich don't pay their fair share, the government won't be able to give the rest of society a fair chance – the rich will keep getting richer, and the poor will never be able to catch up with them.

My way means people are free to do what they want!

Your way means people are free to be poor and sick and uneducated! To have real freedom they have to get a fair chance in life.

LEFT AND RIGHT

Where did 'left' and 'right' come from? The terms were first applied to politics during the French Revolution. In the national assembly, those who wanted to keep the king in charge sat to the right of the chairman, while those who wanted more democracy sat to the left. And the labels stuck!

HOW TO DISAGREE

YOU MAY NOT BE ABLE TO VOTE UNTIL YOU ARE 18, BUT THAT DOESN'T MEAN YOU CAN'T MAKE YOUR VOICE HEARD. IF THERE IS SOMETHING YOU FEEL STRONGLY ABOUT, DON'T JUST COMPLAIN ABOUT IT – TRY TO CHANGE IT!

You can start by telling those in charge how you feel, whether it's your local council, your school, a company or a government department. Say, for example, you think your area needs a new bicycle lane so you can cycle to school more safely. How would you go about trying to get one?

You could start by sending an email to your local authority. But what would you say? Perhaps you could begin by saying who you are, and where you live, and why you would like a cycle lane. Point out the benefits of having one – for instance, it would help people to stay healthy, it would improve road safety and it would be better for the environment.

You'll need to do some research to get the facts you need – maybe you could find out about another area that got a new cycle lane. Did more people take up cycling? Were there fewer cars on the road as a result? Were people happy with the change?

You could make the same arguments to your local politicians. In this case, councillors are the ones who make the decisions, but your local TDs can help too. You could email or write to them – their office addresses will be on the local authority or Dáil website. Even better, you can phone them or go to speak to them directly. Most politicians meet their constituents at regular 'clinics'.

Remember to write down what you want to say beforehand so you won't forget to put your points across. And don't worry that you are too young to vote – a smart politician knows that you will have a vote in a few years and you'll remember if they helped you. And, besides, the adults in your life have a vote already!

You can make your voice louder by getting more people involved. Perhaps you can get them to sign a petition or come along to a public meeting. The more people that are concerned about an issue, the more likely it is that those in charge will treat it seriously.

HOLD A DEBATE!

If you're going to change the world, you have to be able to change people's minds. And to do that, you need some debating skills. So why not try it out? Your teacher might be happy to let you hold a debate in class.

Debating is different from just arguing because there are rules, with time limits on how long you can speak. And you'll need to find out about the issue you are debating so you can make good points. Even if you don't agree with the side your team is on, you still have to present your argument as well as you can.

For a debate, you'll need to have what's called a 'motion' – the statement that you are discussing. Some examples of motions are: 'School uniforms are a good idea', 'Zoos should be banned', or 'Computer games are good for us'.

You'll need two teams (usually with three on each side), one team to argue in favour and one to argue against. The debate starts with the captain of the team in favour of the motion, followed by the captain of the other team, and so on.

The teams need to research the question and come up with different arguments for each speaker.

At the end of the debate, the rest of the class can vote for the team they think made the best argument. And remember – you have to stay polite, even when you are having a debate!

COMHAIRLE NA NÓG

Each local authority in the country has a Comhairle na nÓg, a child and youth council that gives children and young people the chance to have a say in the development of local services and policies. Every two years, each Comhairle na nÓg sends representatives to Dáil na nÓg, the national parliament for children aged 12 to 18.

In 2019, to mark the centenary of the foundation of Dáil Éireann, Dáil na nÓg was held in Leinster House, in the Dáil chamber, and focused on one of the most important issues facing young people – climate change. Perhaps some of the children who sat in the Dáil chamber will be back in those seats one day, making the decisions that affect us all. You can find out more about Comhairle na nÓg and Dáil na nÓg on the website www.comhairlenanog.ie.

WHAT ARE THE BIG ISSUES?

We've looked at who gets to decide and how they decide. But there's another important question — what gets decided? Which issues should be decided by the government, or voters, and which should be left up to people to decide for themselves?

The government gets involved in lots of areas of our lives for very good reasons — to make us healthier, or better educated, or to prevent discrimination. But any time the government makes a rule, it reduces our freedom to do what we want. The question is whether that limit is worth it.

Take the food we eat. It seems sensible that there should be rules to protect people from being poisoned. But what about food that is bad for us if we eat too much of it — like sweets or sugary drinks? Should the government put a limit on how many cans of fizzy drinks we have per week? Or put a tax on sugar to discourage us from using too much? Or should we be able to decide for ourselves how many sweets we eat?

It's clear that we need laws to stop people or companies harming others. There need to be limits on how much pollution a factory can create, for instance, and bans on people being treated unfairly because of their gender or the colour of their skin.

But sometimes people just need more information to make better decisions. After all, if you knew those extra sweets could rot your teeth and make you unhealthy, you'd cut down — wouldn't you?

CIVIL LIBERTIES

THERE IS AN OLD SAYING THAT YOUR RIGHT TO SWING YOUR FIST ENDS WHERE MY NOSE BEGINS. IN OTHER WORDS, YOU HAVE A RIGHT TO DO WHAT YOU WANT, AS LONG AS YOU DON'T INJURE SOMEONE ELSE.

Take smoking, for instance. We know that smoking is *very* bad for you – it can give you diseases that make you very sick or even kill you. So most people don't smoke. But what about people who keep smoking, even though they know it's dangerous? Should they have the freedom to do something that can harm them? The answer in most countries is yes. If someone is old enough, they are allowed to smoke. But increasingly, they are not allowed to smoke where it can harm other people.

Because tobacco smoke can cause disease in people even if they are not smoking themselves, it has been banned in workplaces in Ireland since 2004, including pubs and restaurants. And since 2016, it is illegal to smoke in a car with a child in it. Some smokers claim that this takes away their rights – but while they may have a right to damage their own health, the laws are there to make sure they don't harm anyone else.

People also have a right to protest, to demonstrate against something they think is wrong – like a new government policy. But they don't have the right to use violence in their protest – to throw stones, or burn down buildings, or get into fights with people who disagree with them.

FREEDOM OF SPEECH

The same applies to freedom of speech. You have a right to say what you want, as long as it doesn't harm anyone else. If you were in a crowded shop and you shouted that there was a fire when there wasn't, people might get hurt in the rush to get out.

Your words could also hurt people in other ways – if you said something untrue about them, you could make other people see them differently. For instance, if you fell out with your friend and told other people in your class that they stole something from you, your classmates would be less likely to trust them in future.

If someone thinks they have been damaged by something said or written by another person, they can take them to court to try to get **COMPENSATION** – money to make up for the harm they've suffered. And governments can make it illegal to say bad things about groups of people because of their religion or the colour of their skin.

The problem is deciding how to prevent harmful material *without* squashing freedom of speech. Sometimes people say the government should do something about false information, especially when it is posted online. But who decides what is wrong information? What happens if a government decides that criticism of itself is 'fake news' and forces its removal? It wouldn't be long before nobody could criticise the government, which might be good for the government but not for everyone else.

So any controls on free speech, or other freedoms, need to be carefully thought through, with some way of making sure they aren't abused.

COVID-19

The difficulty of limiting people's freedom in order to protect the health of others was highlighted when the Covid-19 pandemic spread around the world in 2020. Most people accepted that restrictions on their movements were necessary. But some people did not. They argued that, while there might be a case for making infected people stay at home to stop spreading the disease, there shouldn't be rules stopping people who were Covid-free from being out and about.
What do you think?

WOMEN'S RIGHTS

AT THE START OF THE LAST CENTURY, WOMEN HAD TO FIGHT FOR THE RIGHT TO VOTE. BUT GETTING THAT RIGHT DIDN'T MEAN THAT WOMEN BECAME FULLY EQUAL. EVEN TODAY, WOMEN ARE UNDER-REPRESENTED IN POLITICS AND IN BUSINESS LEADERSHIP AND DON'T EARN AS MUCH AS MEN.

That's the bad news. But there is some good news too. Women are more likely to have a third-level education, less likely to go to prison and, of course, they live longer – a girl born in 2012 can expect to live to be almost 83, but a boy's life expectancy is just over 78.

THE MOTHERHOOD GAP

It is illegal to pay someone less just because of their gender. So why do women earn less on average? It may be partly because of what is sometimes called the **MOTHERHOOD GAP**. Women often take time out of their jobs when they have children and are more likely to work part-time to look after them. So, the argument goes, they are less likely to be promoted and therefore earn less.

Many people see this as a pretty poor argument. They argue that raising children shouldn't be the responsibility of women alone – men should do some of it too, and the state should ensure quality childcare is available so women can continue to work.

WOMEN IN POLITICS

The political system has been slow to sort out issues like this, which seems a bit strange. After all, women make up half the electorate, so shouldn't they be able to elect enough women to make decisions that help them? But, in fact, women are still very under-represented in our politics.

After the 2020 general election, only 36 of the 160 TDs were women – less than a quarter. And while it is the highest proportion of women ever elected in Ireland, we don't compare very well with other countries on gender balance in parliament – in October 2020, we were 92nd in the world out of 193 countries. And we've been falling in the world rankings – back in 1990, we were 37th in the world. Other countries have done much better than Ireland in electing more women.

To try to improve things, gender quotas were introduced in 2012 – unless 30 per cent of a political party's candidates were women, they would lose their state funding. This target is due to increase to 40 per cent in 2023. This has helped to elect more women, but there is still a long way to go – and some people don't like the idea of quotas at all.

CONSTANCE MARKIEVICZ

Constance Markievicz was the first woman in an Irish cabinet – she was Minister for Labour in the Dáil cabinet during the War of Independence in 1919. It was another 60 years until the second woman was appointed – Máire Geoghegan-Quinn, who was made Minister for the Gaeltacht in 1979. In the government elected in 2020, four of the fifteen members of cabinet are women.

Women should make up half the decision-makers.

If they were interested, they'd get elected – half the voters are women, so they could choose to elect other women.

If they can't see it, they can't be it – if people aren't used to seeing women in the Dáil, they won't vote for female candidates. The only way to get over the problem is with quotas.

But I want to be elected because I'm the best candidate, not just because I'm a woman!

IMMIGRATION AND ETHNIC MINORITIES

FOR MOST OF THE TIME SINCE INDEPENDENCE, IRELAND WAS RELATIVELY POOR. THERE WEREN'T MANY JOBS, AND MANY PEOPLE LEFT THE ISLAND FOR A BETTER LIFE ABROAD. HALF A MILLION PEOPLE LEFT BETWEEN 1945 AND 1960, MAINLY TO BRITAIN AND AMERICA, AND EMIGRATION ROSE AGAIN IN THE 1980s.

But from the mid-1990s, things changed. With a growing economy and increasing prosperity, Ireland needed more workers and became an attractive place to come to. Back in 1991, just over 190,000 non-Irish nationals were living in the state, mostly from the UK. But 25 years later, in 2016, that figure had grown to more than half a million – just over one in ten of all the people in the state.

Anyone from Britain or the European Union, as well as Switzerland, Iceland, Liechtenstein and Norway, can live and work here without any restrictions. People from other countries have to get permission to come to Ireland and to work here.

REFUGEES

Some people come to Ireland from abroad as **ASYLUM SEEKERS**, looking for protection as refugees. A **REFUGEE** is someone in danger of being badly treated in their own country because of their race, religion, nationality, political opinions or membership of a particular social group.

Under international law, Ireland has to allow them to stay – but only if they are able to prove that they face real danger of bad treatment at home. Asylum seekers who are refused refugee status can be **DEPORTED**, or sent back to their home country.

IRISH CITIZENSHIP

Being an Irish citizen is pretty useful. It allows you to live and work anywhere in the European Union and the UK, and to visit around 170 countries without needing to get a visa (an official stamp in your passport giving you permission to enter a country).

People living legally in Ireland for five years can apply to become Irish citizens, as can the child of an Irish citizen or anyone who had a grandparent born on the island of Ireland.

IRELAND OF THE WELCOMES?

Many people welcome new arrivals into Ireland because they bring benefits for society and the economy. Others think it's only fair to let people come here because many Irish people over the years went to live and work in other countries. Like those Irish emigrants in Britain and America, many people who move here work hard, especially in important areas like health care, and they bring their music, their culture and, of course, their food! But some people don't like immigrants, perhaps because they sometimes look or act differently. Treating people unfairly because of their skin colour or background is called **RACISM**.

This isn't just a problem facing immigrants. Members of the Irish Traveller community also face discrimination in many aspects of life. There are around 30,000 Travellers in the state; in 2017, the government recognised them as a distinct ethnic group. Campaigners said this recognition won more respect for their cultural identity.

TOP TEN NON-IRISH NATIONALITIES

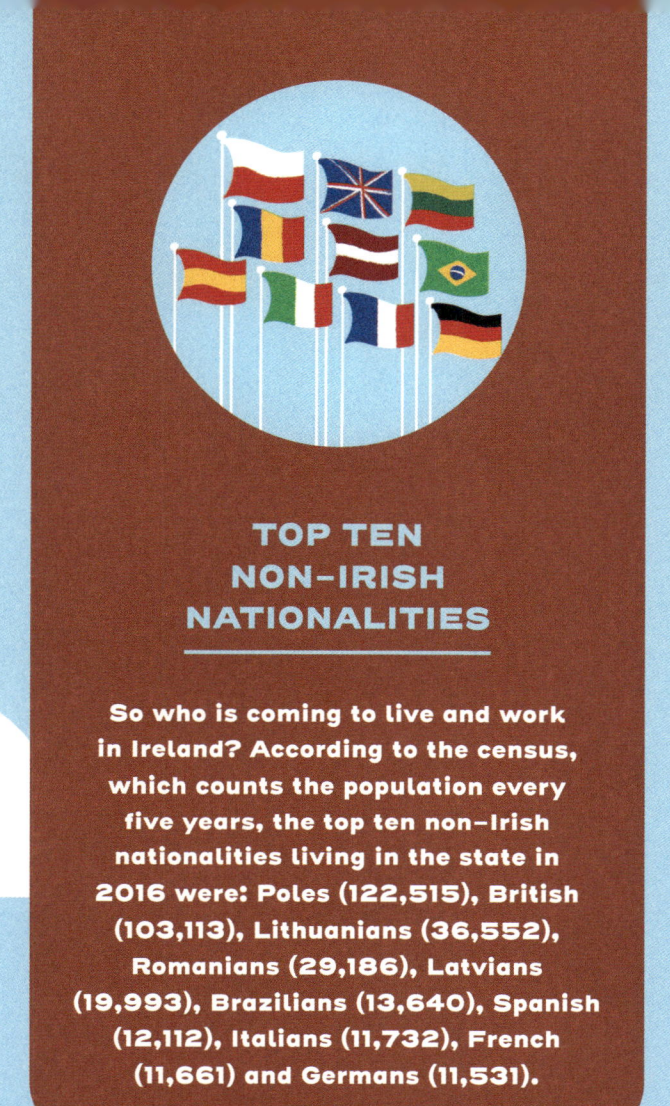

So who is coming to live and work in Ireland? According to the census, which counts the population every five years, the top ten non-Irish nationalities living in the state in 2016 were: Poles (122,515), British (103,113), Lithuanians (36,552), Romanians (29,186), Latvians (19,993), Brazilians (13,640), Spanish (12,112), Italians (11,732), French (11,661) and Germans (11,531).

Discriminating against somebody – by refusing them a job or refusing to serve them in a shop, for instance – because of their race, or because they are a Traveller, or because of gender or religion or having a disability, is against the law.

HOMELESSNESS

WHY DO SOME PEOPLE NOT HAVE A HOME TO LIVE IN? HOMELESSNESS HAS BEEN A GROWING PROBLEM IN IRELAND, AND IT RAISES LOTS OF QUESTIONS ABOUT HOW FAIR OUR SOCIETY IS.

There have always been some people who are homeless, usually through bad luck. Some of these people have problems with alcohol or drug use; some have issues with their mental health; some have seen their relationships break down; some have lost their jobs and aren't able to buy or rent somewhere to live.

But all homeless people have this in common: they have no permanent place to live. Some end up living on the streets, sleeping rough. There are services that try to help them and hostels where they can sleep, but that can't replace a real home.

THE HOUSING CRISIS

In recent years, there has been a different sort of homelessness, which affects families as well as individuals. The price of buying a house has gone up because fewer houses have been built at a time when the population is growing. And the cost of renting somewhere to live has gone up as well. This means that paying for a place to live has got beyond the reach of some people, even if they are working.

The government tries to help people who are homeless by paying some of their rent or finding them a hotel room to stay in for a short time. But hotel rooms are designed for short stays – they aren't suitable for a family to live in because they can't cook their dinner there, they don't have things like washing machines, and there isn't enough space for children to do their homework. And the family may not know how long they can stay in a particular room.

Another type of accommodation is provided in family hubs. Living there is more reliable than staying in a hotel, and families should have play space for their children and be able to cook and do their own laundry. But, again, this is not a real home, and families are only supposed to stay in hubs for a couple of months before a permanent house or apartment becomes available. The only real solution is to build more houses and make them affordable for people to buy or rent.

The Covid-19 pandemic made things worse (it made nearly *everything* worse!). Because of lockdowns designed to stop the spread of the virus, a lot of building work stopped, so fewer houses were built.

Different political parties have different ideas about how to increase the number of houses and apartments being built, depending on whether the party is left or right wing. Some say the government itself should do the building work; others say private builders should do it. But all agree that we need more homes. However, building them takes time and costs money. And with more and more people looking for somewhere to live, the number of new homes needed is increasing all the time.

HOW CAN I HELP?

You may not be able to build a house, but you can still do things to help.

For instance, you could raise money for a homeless charity, maybe by organising a fundraiser with your friends or family. Lots of charities, such as Threshold, Focus Ireland and the Peter McVerry Trust, do very good work helping people.

Some charities collect clothes or toys to help homeless families. Make sure any donations are in good condition – or, even better, new.

And you can let your local politicians know that you are worried about this issue and would like them to take action on it.

CLIMATE CHANGE

POLITICS DECIDES LOTS OF VERY IMPORTANT THINGS – BUT FEW OF THESE ISSUES ARE AS VITAL AS TACKLING CLIMATE CHANGE BECAUSE THE FUTURE OF LIFE ON OUR PLANET DEPENDS ON IT. YET VOTERS DON'T PUT THE ISSUE ANYWHERE NEAR THE TOP OF THEIR CONCERNS WHEN DECIDING WHO TO VOTE FOR, AND POLITICIANS SEEM SLOW TO TAKE REAL ACTION.

Politics sometimes isn't very good at dealing with long-term problems. To prevent something bad in the future – like global warming – you have to do something unpopular now – like increasing taxes on petrol. And sometimes voters are more annoyed by the short-term pain, which they can feel *now*, than impressed by the long-term gain, which they won't see for many years. And politicians need votes to get elected.

A GLOBAL PROBLEM

Climate change is a global problem that needs a worldwide solution. A country won't be protected from climate change by reducing its own greenhouse gases if other countries don't do the same.

But how can this be done fairly?

For instance, since the Industrial Revolution began in 1760, richer countries have been able to develop their economies, making their citizens better off, while pumping greenhouse gases into the atmosphere and contributing to global warming. So how can they now tell *poorer* countries that they can't do the same?

Developing countries fear they will lose the chance to make their people better off if they can't establish industries that might cause pollution. Is that fair? Or should they be allowed to increase their greenhouse gas emissions a bit to allow for economic development, while richer countries agree to extra cuts to their emissions to make up for their past pollution?

And how can the burden be shared fairly *within* countries? Cutting emissions means that some industries won't survive, so people will lose their jobs. Other jobs will be created by new technologies, but people may not be able to switch jobs easily, as the skills needed might be different. There are winners and losers to any kind of change – the question is how to be fair about it, to make what is called a **JUST TRANSITION** to a greener economy.

THE PARIS AGREEMENT

Various attempts have been made to reach a worldwide deal on cutting greenhouse gas emissions. The latest was agreed by members of the United Nations in 2015 in Paris. The aim of the Paris Agreement is to keep the average increase in global temperatures to well below 2 degrees above pre-industrial levels, and to try to reduce the increase to 1.5 degrees.

This is the most ambitious attempt yet to fight climate change, but many people are worried that it isn't ambitious enough. They say the promised reductions in greenhouse gas emissions won't keep the temperature increase below the upper limit of 2 degrees and that even those promises won't be met because there is no way of enforcing them – countries have said they'll do certain things, but there is no penalty if they fail.

Like people, countries don't like being told what to do. But when it comes to climate change, we really are all in this together.

IMPORTANT OR URGENT?

People – including politicians – tend to confuse the important with the urgent. Dwight Eisenhower was one of the top American generals during the Second World War and went on to become President of the United States. So he knew a thing or two about dealing with problems. In 1954, he said, 'I have two kinds of problems: the urgent and the important. The urgent are not important, and the important are never urgent.'

What he meant was that problems that are urgent – that need a decision immediately – tend to crowd out the things that are really important. So we spend our time dealing with immediate tasks instead of concentrating on really vital questions, like ensuring the future of our planet.

EDUCATION

YOU ARE GOING TO SPEND A *LOT* OF TIME GETTING AN EDUCATION. BY THE TIME YOU ARE 18, YOU'LL PROBABLY HAVE SPENT 14 YEARS IN SCHOOL, AND MOST OF YOU WILL GO ON TO THIRD LEVEL AS WELL.

There has been a huge increase in the number of people who continue their education after the Leaving Cert. In 1991, 13.6 per cent of all those aged over 15 had a third-level qualification – that's around one in every seven people. By 2016, the proportion had risen to 42 per cent.

A RIGHT TO EDUCATION

Under the law, you can leave school when you are 16 or have finished three years of secondary school. So why do so many of us stay so much longer? It's not as if learning is so easy. Thanks to Covid-19, lots of parents found out what it was like to teach their kids at home. And it turned out that most of them didn't like it. At all. Many of their children weren't too impressed either.

But while many parents know how hard teaching is and don't want to be teachers themselves, most of them recognise the *value* of education. And society does too. The United Nations and the Council of Europe both say that everyone has the right to an education, and the Constitution has an entire article about education. This says that parents have a right and a duty to provide for the education of their children. And it requires the government to provide for free primary education.

FREE EDUCATION?

Despite being 'free', sending you to school still costs money – things like books, uniforms, transport and after-school activities have to be paid for. Insurance company Zurich estimates the cost of primary school at €1,101 a year, secondary school (without any fees) at €1,891 per year, and college at €4,522 per year (living away from home adds an extra €4,000 per year). So at a *minimum* it will cost €37,514 to get you from Junior Infants to your degree.

Education also costs the government money – building schools and paying teachers. But there are good arguments for spending that money because investing in education makes the economy grow.

The more well-educated workers there are in a country, the more attractive that country is for companies who want to start up new businesses. This is one of the reasons Ireland gets a lot of foreign companies investing here and creating jobs. Also, students who have more education tend to earn higher wages when they enter the workforce. Therefore, they pay more tax – so the money invested in education by government is repaid.

But it's not just about economics. Education also helps us unlock our potential. Learning to read opens up whole new worlds to us, through books or the internet. Being able to do even very simple sums helps us to navigate everyday life. And discovering how society works makes us better citizens and more informed voters.

IS EDUCATION WORTH IT?

According to the 2016 census, people who left school before the age of 16 were twice as likely to be unemployed as those who left later. And incomes were higher as the level of education increased. On average, someone with an honours college degree earned twice as much as someone who left education after the Leaving Cert. And someone with a PhD (that's a doctorate – a degree you do after your ordinary degree) earned nearly five times as much as someone who didn't go further than primary school. That is a big difference. Maybe you'd better stop reading this book and go and do your homework.

HEALTH CARE

GOVERNMENTS DO LOTS OF IMPORTANT THINGS, BUT ONE OF THE MOST IMPORTANT IS RUNNING THE HEALTH SERVICE. IT IS, LITERALLY, A MATTER OF LIFE AND DEATH.

The importance of the health service was highlighted by the Covid-19 pandemic, when the system came very close to being overwhelmed. Health-care workers were under incredible pressure and working very hard, and they also faced the danger of catching the virus themselves and becoming seriously ill or even dying. The people who kept the doors of our hospitals open and kept providing care to the sick through it all were heroes, each and every one of them – nurses, doctors, hospital porters, cleaners, ambulance drivers and others.

But as well as showing the dedication of so many health-care workers, the pandemic highlighted some of the problems with the system – problems that existed before anyone had ever heard of Covid-19. For starters, we don't have enough hospital beds to cater for everyone who needs treatment. There are plans to increase the number, but it takes time to provide extra beds – and, just as important, the staff to go with them.

And the system is short of some important types of health-care workers – intensive-care nurses, for instance, as well as some senior doctors, called consultants.

PUBLIC AND PRIVATE

One of the biggest criticisms of our health service is that there are two systems. The public system is free, but people usually have to wait for treatment because of the shortage of beds and staff. There is also private health care, which allows people with health insurance to get treated more quickly. Many people think this is unfair and that your chances of getting medical treatment shouldn't depend on how much money you have.

There is a plan to reform the health system, called Sláintecare, which is backed by all the parties in the Dáil. Changing the system is expected to take a decade, but if it works, Ireland will have a health service that gives everyone equal access with better results and lower costs.

Of course, staying healthy isn't just about hospital beds or medicines – it's much better not to get sick in the first place. And medical experts say we can do a lot to help ourselves – by keeping as active as we can, by eating well and by minding our mental health.

LIVING LONGER

A baby girl born in 1922, the year the Irish Free State was established, could expect to live to the age of 59.9; a boy's life expectancy was slightly higher, at 60.24. A century later, and life expectancy has soared, to 78.4 for men, and 82.8 for women.

WHAT IS OUR PLACE IN THE WORLD?

In this book, we've seen how individuals can't survive on their own — they need to work together to make society function.

The same applies to countries, which need to co-operate if they want to trade with each other, if they want to tackle climate change and if they want to prevent war.

There are rules about how countries should behave and, just like with people, it makes life easier for everyone if governments follow the rules.

Sometimes countries refuse to do this and try to make themselves stronger by grabbing what doesn't belong to them, usually from a weaker country. Then the international community needs to come together to make sure any countries that break the rules are punished. Otherwise, stronger countries would always be able to do what they want, and weaker countries would suffer.

Imagine the world is like a school playground at break time. If the bigger kids were able to do what they wanted, and take what they wanted, it wouldn't be much fun for the smaller ones, would it? Just like people, countries can sometimes be selfish or greedy and behave badly. And just like in daily life, there have to be rules for how countries behave and punishments for those who break those rules.

THE UNITED NATIONS

THE UNITED NATIONS (UN) WAS SET UP AFTER THE SECOND WORLD WAR. NEARLY EVERY COUNTRY IN THE WORLD BELONGS TO THE UN – MORE THAN 190 OF THEM.

The main aims of the United Nations are to keep the world peaceful; to encourage friendly relations between countries; and to help countries co-operate to improve living standards and respect human rights.

Each of the member states is represented at UN headquarters in New York, where they discuss problems and decide how to deal with them. The people who do this are called **DIPLOMATS** – people sent from their countries to agree on how to solve problems with the diplomats of other countries. A diplomat who represents their nation in another country is called an **AMBASSADOR**, who operates out of an **EMBASSY**. Ireland has embassies in more than 60 countries.

The UN is active on climate change, on economic development in poorer countries, on tackling diseases like malaria and AIDS, on helping refugees, on responding to natural disasters like earthquakes and, most importantly, on trying to stop wars.

If there is an argument between two countries, the UN will try to help them reach an agreement. Sometimes, the dispute can be taken to the International Court of Justice, a branch of the UN.

If one country is trying to bully another or is being unreasonable, the members of the UN might agree to impose **ECONOMIC SANCTIONS** – these are ways of punishing a country for misbehaving. For instance, the UN might ban all other member states from buying a country's products or from selling that country guns.

PEACEKEEPING

If a war does break out, the UN will try to stop the fighting and will sometimes send soldiers to keep the two sides apart. They are called **PEACEKEEPERS**, and although they are members of the armies of the different member states, while they are serving with the United Nations they follow orders from the UN, not their own governments.

Peacekeeping can be a dangerous job, but soldiers serving with the UN have helped to save the lives of many people over the years.

HOW IS THE UN ORGANISED?

There are two main parts of the UN – the General Assembly and the Security Council.

Each of the member states has a vote in the **GENERAL ASSEMBLY**, which discusses all kinds of issues affecting the world. Important decisions need the support of two-thirds of members.

The **SECURITY COUNCIL** tries to keep the peace of the world. There are 15 members – five of the most powerful countries (the United States of America, Russia, China, Britain and France) are permanent members, and each of them must agree before the Security Council takes action. The other ten members are elected by the other countries every two years. It can be very difficult to get the United Nations to take action, especially if one of the permanent members of the Security Council disagrees.

The UN also has its own staff, headed up by the Secretary-General, who is responsible to the member states for what he or she does as the public face and voice of the organisation.

IRELAND AND THE UN

Ireland joined the UN in 1955 and soon took part in its first peacekeeping missions. Because we are neutral (we don't have an agreement to join any other country in a war) and never had an empire, Irish troops are acceptable as peacekeepers in many parts of the world. More than 80 Irish soldiers have died while taking part in peacekeeping missions overseas. Irish troops can only take part in missions that have been approved by the government, the Dáil and the United Nations, a requirement known as the triple lock.

THE EUROPEAN UNION

TWICE IN THE 20TH CENTURY, EUROPE WAS DEVASTATED BY FIGHTING – IN THE FIRST WORLD WAR (1914–18) AND THE SECOND WORLD WAR (1939–45). PEOPLE SAID IT MUST NEVER BE ALLOWED TO HAPPEN AGAIN. BUT HOW COULD WAR BE PREVENTED?

One answer was to tie the economies of the two main European rivals – France and Germany – so closely together that it would be impossible for them to fight each other ever again.

The European Economic Community began in 1958 with six members, and over the years it grew *wider*, taking in more countries, and *deeper*, with agreed policies and rules covering more and more areas of economic and political life. In 2009, it was renamed the European Union. The EU now has 27 member states, with a population of almost 450 million people. Nineteen of the member states use the common currency, the euro.

The member states are still independent countries, but they agree to follow the same laws and policies in some areas. The Common Agricultural Policy helps farmers throughout the EU; regional funds try to help poorer areas catch up with richer regions; and the member states work together on trade deals with other countries.

THE SINGLE MARKET

At the heart of the European Union is the **SINGLE MARKET**, which allows goods, people, services and money to move freely between member states – these are called the **FOUR FREEDOMS**.

This means that an Italian farmer can sell their cheese in Sweden without paying any customs duties and without any health checks because all producers in the EU follow the same rules. A French family can move to live and work in Greece without having to get any special permits. A Belgian construction company can build a road for the Hungarian government. And a Bulgarian citizen can invest in a Danish company because money (also known as **CAPITAL**) can move freely as well.

SEPARATION OF POWERS

Just like the separation of powers in most countries, power in the European Union is divided. There is the **EUROPEAN PARLIAMENT**, whose members are elected by the citizens of each member state. Each country gets a share of MEPs (Members of the European Parliament) in proportion to their population – the more people in a country, the more MEPs it has. The parliament passes laws and approves the members of the commission.

The **EUROPEAN COMMISSION** is responsible for carrying out policies. Each member state nominates one commissioner, who is then given a particular area to look after, a bit like a minister in our own government.

But most of the really important decisions are taken by the **EUROPEAN COUNCIL**, where the governments of all the member states are represented.

There is also a **COURT OF JUSTICE**, which decides whether European law has been correctly followed by the Commission or member states' governments.

BREXIT

In 2020, Britain became the first member state to leave the EU, after a referendum in 2016. The British exit – known as Brexit – meant that it would no longer have to follow the rules agreed by a majority of member states. But it also meant that it became more difficult to sell British products to the EU and to import European products into Britain.

PROS AND CONS

There has never been an organisation like the European Union, where so many countries have agreed to co-operate so closely in so many areas. Sometimes it can be too slow to react in a crisis; sometimes it can be selfish, looking after its own interests at the expense of poorer countries; sometimes it fails to take action against member states that break the rules; sometimes it can seem remote from ordinary citizens.

But it has made trade easier, made many citizens better off and allowed Europeans to travel freely around the continent. Most of all, it has made war between the member states unthinkable.

HUMAN RIGHTS

WE SAW ON PAGE 42 THAT OUR CONSTITUTION GIVES CITIZENS CERTAIN RIGHTS. BUT WHAT HAPPENS IF A COUNTRY FAILS TO RESPECT THE RIGHTS OF ITS CITIZENS? WHERE CAN THEY GO TO GET JUSTICE?

Since the end of the Second World War, more attention has been given to the idea of **UNIVERSAL HUMAN RIGHTS**, which everyone in the world should be able to enjoy, and to giving people a way of making sure those rights are respected, even if they are opposed by their own government.

THE UNIVERSAL DECLARATION OF HUMAN RIGHTS

On 12 December 1948, the United Nations General Assembly adopted the **UNIVERSAL DECLARATION OF HUMAN RIGHTS**, which says that everyone is born free and equal and is entitled to the same rights, no matter who they are, who their parents are, what language they speak or their gender, religion, nationality, political opinions or race.

The Universal Declaration says we all have the right to life and to live in freedom and safety. We have the right to be treated the same way by the law, to be seen as innocent until proven guilty and to have a fair trial. We have the right to privacy, to freedom of movement, to a nationality, to get married and have a family, to own property, to believe what we want and to choose our own government. We have the right to education, to fair pay for our work, to have time off and holidays, and to enjoy the arts. And we all have the right to be free from slavery and from torture and from being put in prison unfairly.

That is a *lot* of rights, and if governments around the world followed the Universal Declaration, people could be sure they would be treated fairly. But unfortunately, many governments do not do this, and many people are denied the rights set out in the Universal Declaration. Nobody has the power to enforce the declaration in another country; the best the United Nations can do is highlight rights that are being denied and hope that the pressure of international opinion will make governments do the right thing.

EUROPEAN CONVENTION ON HUMAN RIGHTS

This is a bit of a problem – after all, if a government is prepared to mistreat its citizens, it probably won't care very much if it is criticised by other countries. This flaw was recognised by European politicians, who agreed to go one better with the **EUROPEAN CONVENTION ON HUMAN RIGHTS**, which from the beginning included a court that could find against governments if they infringed the rights of their own citizens.

MALALA YOUSAFZAI

In 2014, 17-year-old Malala Yousafzai became the youngest person to win the Nobel Peace Prize. Malala, who is from Pakistan, campaigns for the right of girls to education. She survived an assassination attempt in 2012 by religious fundamentalists who don't believe girls should go to school. Malala refused to give in to their violence and went on to give a speech at the United Nations that brought her campaign to world attention. The gunmen tried to silence her, but because of their actions, her message was spread to many more people.

The European Convention on Human Rights was adopted in 1950 by the Council of Europe (which is a separate organisation to the European Union, with more members but less power). One of the people who helped draw up the convention was the Irish minister Seán MacBride.

Since then, citizens have been able to take cases to the European Court of Human Rights if they feel they have been treated unfairly by their government. As a result of losing cases at the court, the Irish government has had to change its laws or its behaviour on a number of different issues.

WAR AND PEACE

WAR – FIGHTING BETWEEN THE ARMIES OF TWO OR MORE COUNTRIES – IS REGARDED BY MOST PEOPLE AS THE VERY LAST RESORT WHEN THERE IS AN INTERNATIONAL DISAGREEMENT.

As well as lives being lost, wars cause further unnecessary suffering. People may have to leave their homes to get out of the way of an approaching army, their lives will be disrupted and food may become scarce. Soldiers suffer during wars, but innocent civilians usually suffer even more.

But while war is a last resort, does that mean it is *never* necessary? Some people think so – they are called **PACIFISTS** and believe that no country should fight, even if invaded, and they refuse to serve in the military. But others think there are some circumstances in which war is the only option.

For instance, if a country is invaded by its neighbour, most people would say it has a right to defend itself. But what if a country *thinks* its neighbour is getting too powerful and might invade it in the future? Is it entitled to attack first? Is it entitled to launch a war to prevent another country developing a powerful weapon? Can it justify an invasion to stop another government mistreating its people? These are difficult questions, and there are few easy answers.

Another difficult question is how a war should be fought. Obviously, if you are at war you want to win. But are you allowed to do whatever it takes to do that, or do you have to follow rules?

GENEVA CONVENTIONS

Most countries have signed up to international rules on how they should act during wars, called the **GENEVA CONVENTIONS**. These aim to protect those who are not involved in the war ('civilians') and those who are no longer taking part, like soldiers who have been wounded or captured by their enemy ('prisoners-of-war'). However, despite this, it is not clear if it is against international law to bomb cities, which would kill many civilians. In practice, the Geneva Conventions would offer very little protection if a country at war decided it needed to bomb civilians in order to win.

REVOLUTION

The use of violence is not just about war between countries. Sometimes a government treats its people so badly that they decide to fight to overthrow it in a **REVOLUTION**. Examples of this are the French Revolution of 1789, which overthrew the king and brought in a republic, or the Hungarian Uprising of 1956, which tried to get rid of Communist rule.

Another sort of revolution is against a foreign power that controls a country. Examples of this include the American Revolution of 1776, our own Easter Rising and War of Independence, and numerous revolts against colonial powers in Africa and Asia during the 20th century.

Some of the same questions arise in these situations as in wars between countries. Is the use of violence justified in the first place, and what sort of violence can be used? Sometimes, people use what is called **TERRORISM** – attacking ordinary people to create fear and make it difficult for society to work in the hope that the government will give in to their demands.

Even if a revolution achieves its aims by replacing the government or gaining independence, it usually isn't the end of the story. Many countries, including our own, have seen civil wars after independence, and revolutions seldom end peacefully. It's easy to begin using violence; it's more difficult to stop it.

IRISH NEUTRALITY

Ireland has a policy of military neutrality. This means that we are not a member of any defence alliances, which are agreements between countries to join in a war if any of the other members are involved.

When the Second World War broke out in 1939, our government decided to stay out of it and remain neutral. Most other small countries in Europe tried to do the same, though many of them were unable to stay out of the war because they were invaded. Luckily, neither side invaded Ireland.

INDEX

A
Act of Union (1801), 8, 9
Air Corps, 52
ambassadors, 82
American Revolution (1776), 9, 89
Ancient Egypt, 8
Ancient Greece, 14
Army, 52-3
Army Permanent Defence Forces, 53
Army Ranger Wing, 52
Army Reserve, 53
asylum seekers, 70
Australia, 15, 36, 39
authority, 2-3

B
backbenchers, 18
Belarus, 59
Belgium, 39
Brehon Laws, 7
Brexit, 85
Brian Boru, High King of Ireland, 6
British citizens in Ireland, 38, 71
broadcasters, 54, 55
Broadcasting Authority of Ireland, 54
Budget, 30-1
Bulgaria, 39
Bunreacht na nÉireann *see* Constitution of Ireland

C
Caligula (Roman emperor), 9
Canada, 59
Catholic emancipation (1829), 9
Catholics, and voting rights, 8
Ceann Comhairle, 18
Census (2016), 77
childcare, 68
children
   and Comhairle na nÓg, 63
   and the courts, 49
   and homelessness, 72
   news programme for, 55
China, 83
civil liberties, 66-7
civil servants, 17, 20, 21, 29
clann, 6
clans, 6, 7
climate change, 74-5
co-operation, 3
coalition governments, 22, 58, 60
Collins, Michael, 11
Comhairle na nÓg, 63
compensation, 48, 66
compulsory voting, 39
Constitution of Ireland (1937), 26, 42-3
   the common good, 43
   and education, 76
   equal before the law, 41
   rights of citizens, 42, 43
constitutional referendums, 38, 44-5
Cork City Council, 28, 29
Cosgrave, W.T., 23
Council of Europe, 76, 87
Councillors, 25, 29
county councils, 17, 28
court cases
   civil cases, 48
   criminal cases, 48
Court of Justice of the European Union, 85
courts, 48-9
   and children, 49
   and compensation, 48
   and prison, 49
   and restorative justice, 49
Covid-19 pandemic, 30, 31, 67, 73, 78
Czech Republic, 59

D
Dáil Éireann, 15, 17, 18-19
   backbenchers, 18
   the Ceann Comhairle, 18
   and committees, 19
   and legislation, 26
   and name-calling, 19
   and privilege, 19
   and TDs, 18-19
Dáil elections, 38
Dáil na nÓg (2019), 63
de Valera, Éamon, 11, 23
death penalty, abolition of, 45
debates, 63
Defence Forces, 52-3
   divisions of, 52-3
   mission of, 52
Defence Forces Training Centre, 52
democracy, 5, 14-15
   in Ancient Greece, 14
   direct democracy, 14
   representative democracy, 14
   and voting rights, 14
democratic systems
   federal system, 15
   parliamentary system, 15
   presidential system, 15
   unitary system, 15
Department of Education, 30
Department of Health, 30
Department of Social Protection, 30
deportation, 70
dictatorships, 15, 39
diplomats, 82
discrimination, 71
Dublin City Council, 28, 29
Dublin City University (DCU), 25
Dublin County Councils, 28
dúiche, 6

E
Easter Rising (1916), 10, 52, 89
Eastern Europe, 59
economic sanctions, 82
education, 76-7
   cost of, 77
   and earnings, 77
   free education, 77
   the right to, 76
Éire, 11
Eisenhower, Dwight, 75
elections, 34-5, 38
embassies, 82
ethnic minorities, 70-1
Euro currency, 31, 84
European Commission, 85
European Convention on Human Rights (1950), 51, 86, 87
European Council, 85
European Court of Human Rights, 87
European Economic Community (EEC), 84
European elections, 38

European Parliament, 38
European Union (EU), 31, 84–5
  and Brexit, 85
  Common Agricultural Policy (CAP), 84
  Court of Justice, 85
  the euro, 84
  European Commission, 85
  European Council, 85
  the four freedoms, 84
  member states, 84
  pros and cons, 85
  and referendums, 45
  separation of powers, 85
  the single market, 84

F

Fianna Fáil, 58, 60
Fine Gael, 58, 60
Finucane, Michael, 35
first past the post, 34, 35
First World War (1914–18), 84
Four Courts, 49
France, 14, 83, 84
Frederick William I, King of Prussia, 9
freedom of speech, 54, 66–7
French people in Ireland, 71
French Revolution (1789), 9, 61, 89

G

Gaelic Ireland, 6–7
  and the Brehon Laws, 7
  and clans, 5, 6
  the five provinces of, 6
  and freemen, 7
  and kings, 7
  and the Norman invasion, 7
  and slaves, 7
  and social rank, 7
  and warriors, 7
Galway City Council, 28
Garda College, Templemore, County Tipperary, 50
Garda Dog Unit, 51
Garda Reserve, 50
Garda Síochána, An, 48, 50–1
General Election (1918), 10
General Election (2002), 35
General Election (2020), 69
General elections, 38, 59
Geneva Conventions, 88
Geoghegan-Quinn, Máire, 60
Germans in Ireland, 71
Germany, 15, 84
Good Friday Agreement (1998), 12, 45
government, 2, 3
  borrowing money, 31
  branches of, 46–7
  and the Budget, 30
  and cabinet confidentiality, 21
  coalition governments, 22, 58, 60
  and collective responsibility, 21
  holding government to account, 18
  and taxes, 31
  and vote of confidence, 18
government branches
  executive, 46, 47
  judiciary, 46
  legislature, 46
government departments, 20–1
  and administration, 20
  and policy, 20
  and the Secretary-General, 20

government ministers, 20–1
Greece, 39
Green Party, 58, 60
greenhouse gas emissions, 74, 75

H

health care, 78–9
  and Covid-19 pandemic, 78
  private system, 79
  public system, 79
  shortage of health-care workers, 78
  Sláintecare, 79
health insurance, 79
hereditary monarchs, 8
high kings of Ireland, 6
Hobbes, Thomas, 3
homelessness, 72–3
housing shortage, 72, 73
human rights, 86–7
Hungarian Uprising (1956), 89

I

immigration, 70–1
Income Tax, 31
Independents, 58
India, 36
Industrial Revolution, 74
International Court of Justice, 82
'Ireland's Call', 13
Ireland's flag, 11
Irish citizenship, 71
Irish Civil War (1922–3), 11
Irish Free State, 10, 11, 14
Irish independence, 5, 10–11
Irish Independent online, 55
Irish Volunteers, 52
Italians in Ireland, 71

J

joke political parties, 59
judiciary (courts), 46, 47

K

kings, 6
  the divine right of, 8
Kirkland, James, 9

L

Labour Party, 58, 59
Latvians in Ireland, 71
laws, 41, 49
left and right, origin of terms, 61
left wing, 60
left-winger, 61
Lemass, Seán, 23
life expectancy, 79
Limerick City, 29
Limerick County Council, 28
Lithuanians in Ireland, 71
local authorities, 62, 63
local elections, 38
local government, 28–9
Lonergan, Darcy, 29
Lord Mayor of Dublin, 29
Luxembourg, 39
Lynch, Jack, 23

M

MacBride, Seán, 87
Malta, 36

Markievicz, Constance, 69
Maynooth University, 25
Mayor of Carrickmacross, 29
Mayor of Waterford, 29
Mayors, 29
Meagher, Thomas Francis, 11
media, the, 54–5
  code of practice, 54
Minister for Finance, 30
Minister for Public Expenditure, 30
Ministers, 20–1
  Cabinet Ministers, 20
  Junior Ministers, 20
  Ministers of State, 20
Mint in Sandyford, 31
monarch, 5, 8
monarchy, 8–9
money, 31
Monster Meetings, 9

N

national anthems
  'Amhrán na bhFiann', 13
  'God Save the Queen', 13
National Debt, 31
National University of Ireland (NUI), 25
Nationalists, 12, 13
Naval Service, 53
neutrality, 83, 89
New Zealand, 36
news, 54
news sources, 55
news2day, 55
newspapers, 54
Nobel Peace Prize (2014), 87
non-Irish nationalities in Ireland, 71
Norman invasion (1169), 7
North Korea, 39
Northern Ireland, 10, 12–13
Northern Ireland Assembly, 13
  and the Deputy First Minister, 13
  and the First Minister, 13
  proportional representation (PR-STV), 13
Northern Ireland Executive, 13
NUI Galway, 25

O

O'Connell, Daniel, 9
Official Monster Raving Loony Party, 59
Óglaigh na hÉireann see Defence Forces
Oireachtas, 17, 18, 47

P

pacifists, 88
Pakistan, 36, 87
Paris Agreement (2015), 75
peacekeepers, 83
peacekeeping, 52, 83
Peter the Great, Tsar, 9
pharaohs, 8
plurality voting, 34, 35
Poland, 59
Poles in Ireland, 71
political disagreements, 57
political ideologies, 60–1
political parties, 58–9
  Fianna Fáil, 58
  Fine Gael, 58
  Green Party, 58
  Independents, 58
  joke parties, 59

Labour Party, 58, 59
  the party line, 59
  Sinn Féin, 58
  Social Democrats, 58, 59
  Solidarity/People Before Profit, 58, 59
  and the whip, 59
politicians, 33
politics, 2
  and choices, 33
Potsdam Giants, 9
power, 9
President of Ireland, 17, 18, 26–7
  and age, 27, 44
  guardian of the Constitution, 26–7
  legislation signed by, 26
  symbolic role of, 27
President of the United States, 47
presidential elections, 38, 39
Press Council of Ireland, 54
prison, 49
prisoners-of-war, 88
proportional representation (PR), 34, 35, 36
proportional representation (PR-STV), 36–7
  constitutional referendum on, 44
  example, 37
  non-transferable votes, 37
  and the Northern Ireland Assembly, 13
  quotas, 36
  spoiled votes, 36
  surplus votes distributed, 37
  transfers, 37
provinces of Ireland
  Connacht, 6
  Laighin (Leinster), 6
  Midhe (Meath), 6
  Mumhain (Munster), 6
  Ulaidh (Ulster), 6

R

racism, 71
referendums, 38, 44–5
Reform Act (1850), 8
refugees, 70
Republic of Ireland, 5, 10–11
republicanism, 9, 10
restorative justice, 49
Reuters Digital News Report (2021), 55
revolution, 89
Rhinoceros Party, 59
right and left, origin of terms, 61
right wing, 60
right-winger, 61
rights of citizens, 42–3
Romanians in Ireland, 71
RTÉ News online, 55
RTÉ2, 55
Rugby World Cup (1995), 13
rules, 41
Russia, 9, 59, 83

S

same-sex marriages, 45
school referendum, 45
Seanad, 17, 18, 20, 24–5, 47
  and electors, 25
  and legislation, 26
  and referendum (2013), 24, 44
  Taoiseach's nominations, 25
  university senators, 25
  vocational panels, 24
Seanad vocational panels
  Administrative (7 seats), 24

    Agricultural (11 seats), 24
    Cultural and Educational (5 seats), 24
    Industrial and Commercial (9 seats), 24
    Labour (11 seats), 24
Second World War (1939–45), 11, 75, 84, 89
Senators
    appointed by the Taoiseach, 20, 24, 25
    appointed as ministers, 20
    election of, 24, 25
    number of, 24
separation of powers, 46–7
    executive, 46, 47
    judiciary, 46, 47
    legislature, 46, 47
    in the United States, 47
Serbia, 59
Sinn Féin, 10, 58
Sláintecare, 79
slaves in Gaelic Ireland, 7
smoking, 66
Social Democrats, 58, 59
social media, 55
Solidarity/People Before Profit, 58, 59
Supreme Court, 26
surnames of clan members, 6
Switzerland, 14

T

Taoiseach, 15, 20, 22–3
    and Dáil vote for, 22, 26
    duties of, 22
    how to become, 23
    senators nominated by, 25
taxes, 31, 46
Teachtaí Dála (TDs), 15, 17, 18
Technological University Dublin (TU Dublin), 25
terrorism, 89
TheJournal.ie, 55
Traveller community, 71
tricolour, 11
Trinity College Dublin, 25
Troubles, The, 12

U

Unionists, 12, 13
United Irishmen, 9
United Kingdom of Great Britain and Ireland, 8
    and government, 5
    and Irish independence, 5
    and the monarch, 5
    and Northern Ireland, 13
    and the UN Security Council, 83
United Nations (UN), 82–3
    General Assembly, 83, 86
    and Ireland, 83
    Paris Agreement (2015), 75
    and peacekeeping, 83
    the right to education, 76
    Secretary-General, 83
    Security Council, 83
    Universal Declaration of Human Rights (1948), 86
United States of America (USA), 15, 83
    the executive (President), 47
    legislature (Congress), 47
    separation of powers, 47
Universal Declaration of Human Rights (1948), 86
University College Cork (UCC), 25
University College Dublin (UCD), 25
University of Limerick (UL), 25

V

vote of confidence, 18
voting
    British citizens in Ireland, 38
    compulsory voting, 39
    the Irish abroad, 39
    opportunities, 38
    registration, 38
voting age, 14, 38, 39, 44
voting rights, 14
    and Catholics, 8
    and democracy, 14
    and the Reform Act (1850), 8
    and the secret ballot, 8
    and women, 14
voting systems
    first past the post, 34, 35
    majority system, 34
    mixed system, 35
    plurality system, 34, 35
    proportional representation (PR), 34, 35
    proportional representation (PR-STV), 36–7

W

war, 88–9
    and the Geneva Conventions, 88
    prisoners-of-war, 88
War of Independence (1919–21), 10, 89
warriors in Gaelic Ireland, 7
Waterford City, 29
Waterford County Council, 28
women
    in government, 69
    in politics, 69
    and voting rights, 14
women's rights, 68–9
    and the motherhood gap, 68
Wyse, Adam, 29

Y

Yousafzai, Malala, 87

Z

Zurich Insurance Company, 77

Gill Books
Hume Avenue
Park West
Dublin 12
www.gillbooks.ie

Gill Books is an imprint of M.H. Gill and Co.

Text © David McCullagh 2021
Illustrations © Graham Corcoran 2021
978 07171 90287

Designed by www.grahamthew.com
Edited by Emma Dunne
Proofread by Esther Ní Dhonnacha
Indexed by Eileen O'Neill
Printed by APPL, Aprinta Druck, GmbH, Germany
This book is typeset in 11pt Henderson Sans

The paper used in this book comes from the wood pulp of managed forests.
For every tree felled, at least one tree is planted, thereby renewing natural resources.

All rights reserved.
No part of this publication may be copied, reproduced or transmitted in any form
or by any means, without written permission of the publishers.

A CIP catalogue record for this book is available from the British Library.

5 4 3 2 1

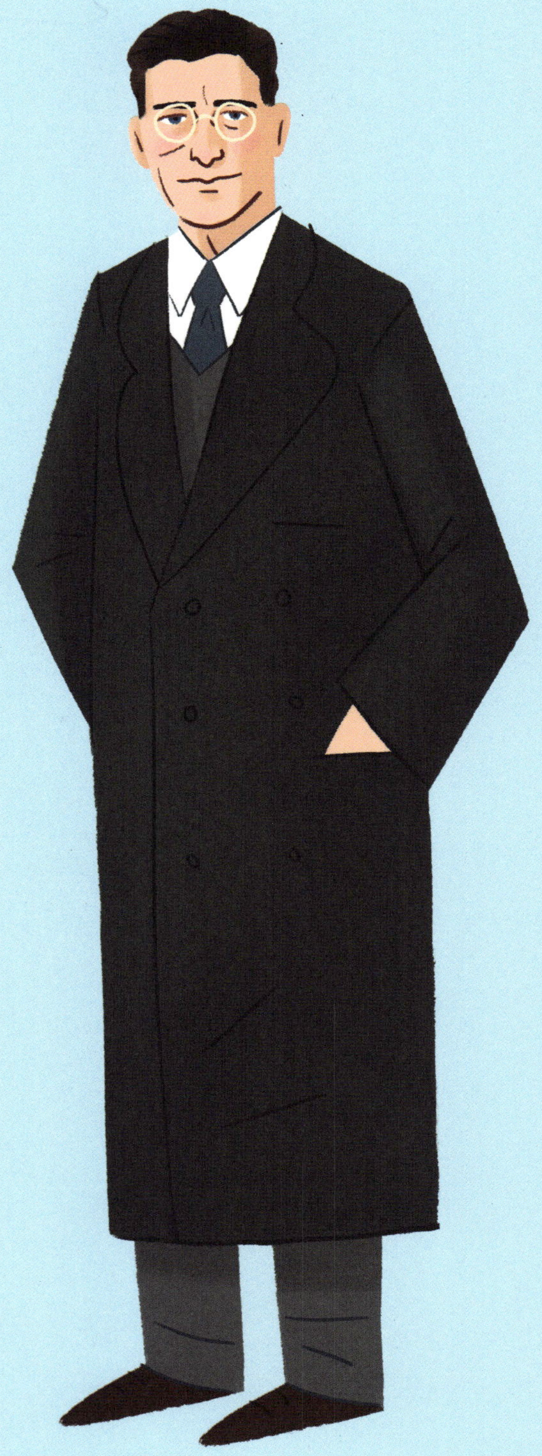